MANAGEMENT
BY
OBJECTIVES

MANAGEMENT
BY
OBJECTIVES

APPLICATIONS AND RESEARCH

STEPHEN J. CARROLL, JR.
Department of Business Administration
University of Maryland

HENRY L. TOSI, JR.
Department of Management
Michigan State University

MACMILLAN PUBLISHING CO., INC.
NEW YORK
COLLIER MACMILLAN PUBLISHERS
LONDON

TO OUR PARENTS:

Stephen J. Carroll
Helene A. Clancy
Henry L. Tosi
Rose M. Tosi

Copyright © 1973, MACMILLAN PUBLISHING CO., INC.
Printed in the United States of America

MACMILLAN PUBLISHING CO., INC.
866 Third Avenue, New York, New York 10022

Collier-Macmillan Canada, Ltd., Toronto, Ontario

Library of Congress catalog card number: 72-75858

Printing   3 4 5 6 7 8   Year   4 5 6 7 8 9

PREFACE

Approximately five years ago, we initiated a management development training program at The Black & Decker Manufacturing Company, a manufacturer of power tools for home, industrial, and construction use. After several management groups had been trained, we began a study of the firm's management by objectives (MBO) program. Simultaneously, we collected data by means of interviews, questionnaires, and input from personnel files and examined the existing literature on the subject of MBO. Eighteen months later we participated in a change program designed to improve the existing Black & Decker MBO program, and then evaluated the results of this change effort. Since that time we have individually conducted various training programs in MBO and have become involved with new research studies on this topic in several other organizations.

Our discussion of the MBO approach in this book is based on our own research and on the few other research studies that have been conducted on this topic. We have described or cited several of these research studies in preference to a discussion or citation of all articles or books written on the subject because we wanted to provide a coverage of the topic based on research results. In addition, our text emphasizes the behavioral aspects of MBO to a greater degree than any other work on the subject; this emphasis reflects our own research orientation.

This book was written to be used in either the academic or the industrial setting. Statistics are presented in the appendixes to the book and in the footnotes; the text itself contains descriptions of research findings made by us and others. The book also contains many suggestions and conclusions made on the basis of our evaluation of the relevant research on this topic. Thus, we hope that the book will be of practical value as well as contribute to future research.

In the academic setting, we see the book used primarily as a supplementary text in a variety of personnel and management courses. In the industrial setting, this book should be of value to all the managers in any firm with an MBO program as well as serve as the textbook in courses on this topic. We have found that most individual managers in organizations with an MBO program need and want guidance in how actually to carry out the MBO process. We hope we have provided this in these pages.

Many individuals have made different types of contributions to this book. At Black & Decker, C. Allen Kozelski, Vice-president of Personnel, Jay Jacobs, Director of Management Planning and Development, and Mary Lou Garrison, Personnel Assistant, were actively involved in the research that we carried out in the firm and contributed much to our thinking about what MBO was and ought to be. Dr. John Rizzo of Western Michigan University made very significant contributions to Chapter 4 in the book. Early reviews of the manuscript by John Miner of the University of Maryland and Stuart Klein of the University of Kentucky were very helpful. Several graduate assistants also contributed to various analyses of the data, including Dennis Cintron of the University of Maryland and Rod Chesser, James Tartar, and Richard Walters of Michigan State University. We also deeply appreciate all the help we received from our former editor, John C. Neifert, of The Macmillan Company. Finally, we would like to thank our various typists, especially Isabel Thompson and Dorothy Vance.

Each of us has contributed equally to this book and to our joint research efforts. We hope that our slight difference in perspectives has enhanced our research.

S. J. C.
H. L. T.

CONTENTS

1
WHAT IS MANAGEMENT BY OBJECTIVES?

"Management by objectives" (MBO), like many other management approaches and techniques, first originated in managerial practice and then was further refined and extended by various researchers and management writers. Peter Drucker is responsible for first publicizing the MBO approach in his *Practice of Management,* written in 1954.[1]*

In his book, Drucker pointed out the advantages of managing by "objectives" rather than managing by "drives." In managing by objectives, he said, each manager from the highest level to the lowest level should have clear objectives that reflect and support the objectives of higher-level management. Drucker also stressed that it is desirable to have every manager help establish higher-level objectives as well as his own. This, Drucker indicated, enables the individual manager to know and understand the goals of his

---

* Supra numbers throughout the book refer to notes at the end of the particular chapter.

organization as well as his superior's expectations with regard to his own performance.

Drucker also described how some effective managers implemented an objectives approach through the use of a "manager's letter." Here a subordinate writes a letter to his superior twice a year in which he defines the objectives of his own and of his superior's job. The subordinate also outlines the plans he will follow in achieving his objectives, the obstacles he expects to face in carrying out his plan, and the aid he will need from others in the organization to overcome the obstacles. When the letter is approved by the superior, it becomes the subordinate's performance guide. Drucker also points out that the letter can reveal misunderstandings between the superior and the subordinate, contradictory performance demands on the subordinate, and organizational problems.

Douglas McGregor also advocated the use of the MBO approach.[2] He pointed out that many performance appraisal programs failed because of resistance to them by both superiors and subordinates and that MBO could be a solution to this problem. He suggested that each manager establish short-term performance goals for himself after first reaching agreement with his superior on his major job responsibilities. Specific plans for achieving the short-term goals would also be established by the subordinate. Then he would appraise his accomplishments at the end of a short period of time, such as six months. This self-appraisal would then be discussed with his superior, after which new short-term performance goals would be established. McGregor argued that this approach was superior to the traditional performance appraisal methods because it gave the subordinate self-insight and shifted the emphasis from an appraisal to identify weaknesses to an analysis of performance to define strengths and potentials. Also, McGregor felt that for the subordinate the MBO approach would redefine the superior's role as that of a helper rather than that of a judge. In addition, he pointed out that this approach would enhance subordinate acceptance more than the traditional procedure because the former emphasizes performance rather than the personality of the subordinate and emphasizes his future actions rather than his past behavior.

McGregor's arguments seemed to be widely accepted, especially among managers. This is evidenced by the wide sales of his book and the favorable reviews of his writings. Practitioners and scholars often mentioned his ideas in their articles on rating and performance, and many companies adopted performance appraisal programs using his approach. McGregor directed attention to MBO more as a performance appraisal technique, whereas Drucker stressed integrating the activities and balancing the objectives of the organization.

THE MBO PROCESS

Although opinions vary on how to use the MBO approach and some persons disagree about its purposes, most authorities in the field agree that this approach involves the establishment and communication of organizational goals, the setting of individual objectives pursuant to the organizational goals, and the periodic and then final review of performance as it relates to the objectives. In addition, agreement would be likely on the following elements as necessary to an effective MBO program:

1. Effective goal setting and planning by top levels of the managerial hierarchy.
2. Organizational commitment to this approach.
3. Mutual goal setting.
4. Frequent performance review.
5. Some degree of freedom in developing means for the achievement of objectives.

Organizations that have implemented these ideas refer to their programs variously as "management by results," "goals management," "work planning and review," "goals and controls," and so on. However, all these programs are similar, despite the differences in terminology.

RESEARCH FOUNDATIONS OF MBO

There is little doubt that the objectives approach makes good sense. However, the use of any managerial approach should be justified by more than its apparent rationality; it should be based on the existing research. As we shall see, there is a considerable body of basic research that does support the core of MBO concepts, but to date the research has tended to deal with only a few aspects of the MBO approach: the setting of goals, feedback or knowledge of results, and subordinate participation in decision making.

GOAL SETTING

Most of the early research in the area of goal setting consisted of level-of-aspiration studies, which described the discrepancy between a previous level of performance and the subject's new proposed level of performance (level of aspiration) as a function of previous success and failure. One of the first and most significant findings in this area is that subjects initially tend to set performance goals at higher levels than previous performance levels and then tend to keep them higher.[3] Thus, most goals established by subjects are progressive ones, generally requiring higher levels of performance. However, if the subjects are unsuccessful in achieving goals, the level of aspiration in following periods is not as high as when the subjects are successful. The degree to which new goals are higher depends upon the degree of success attained in achieving previous goals.[4] Fryer found that forcing subjects to set goals increased the level of performance most when the task was difficult.[5] He also found that the process of goal setting had a larger effect on performance than did a knowledge of results.

Recently a series of highly controlled experimental studies on the effects that goals have on behavior was conducted by Locke and Bryan. Locke and his colleagues, in a series of twelve studies, found that the higher the intended level of achievement, the higher the level of performance.[6] Stedry and Kay, however, found that when supervisors considered very difficult goals impossible instead of challenging, their performance decreased significantly.[7] In six out of eight studies,[8] Locke and Bryan found that specific goals resulted in significantly higher levels of performance than when subjects were merely told to do their best. Locke also found that with boring tasks, setting goals increased interest.[9] Like Fryer, Locke and Bryan found that goal setting itself increases performance more than does feedback alone.[10] That is, it is the goal originally established that produces most of the "motivational force" in the situation rather than the provision of feedback to the subject as to how well he is doing. However, they did find that feedback, when given in relation to standards or expectations, does influence the goal level chosen and therefore subsequent performance.[11] In another study, Bryan and Locke found that employees in an initially "low motivation" group caught up to an initially "high motivation" group when the former were given specific goals to accomplish rather than merely being told to do their best.[12]

The time allowed on a task also influences its difficulty. In two studies, Bryan and Locke found that subjects who were given more time to do a task took more time and set easier goals than subjects given the minimum amount of time necessary for goal success, according to their abilities.[13] Locke and others have also conducted studies that indicate that performance dissatisfaction depends on the relationship of actual performance to one's performance goals.[14] In addition, the research by Locke and Bryan and other research cited by them have indicated that goals and intentions are the primary motivational determinants of task performance and that external incentives influence behavior through their effects on goals and intentions.[15]

DISCUSSION. The research on goal setting indicates that the degree of task performance does depend on whether goals are established. Based on this finding, MBO programs should improve performance whenever there is goal acceptance. How much performance improves will, of course, depend on whether goals are at the appropriate level of difficulty for the individual, whether proper time limits are set, and whether the goals are specific or not. Specific goals direct energy in specific directions and in specific amounts; otherwise, the individual's energy may become diffused among different activities or may be disbursed in insufficient or inefficient amounts. Thus, specific goals enable the individual to calculate the probability of success more easily than vague goals. In addition, as Porter and Lawler, Atkinson and Feather, and others have pointed out, an individual's past experiences with success or failure in reaching certain goals would help determine his perceptions of the probability of success in attaining a present or future goal.[16] The research also shows that harder goals increased performance consistently even when the probability of goal attainment diminished. This, of course, occurred only when the subjects accepted the difficult performance goals established by others. When individuals established low-level personal goals and did not accept harder goals imposed by others, their performance in turn was obviously low.[17]

FEEDBACK OR KNOWLEDGE OF RESULTS

The evidence is quite clear that feedback or knowledge of results can also improve performance. For example, Pryer and Bass gave feedback to thirteen of twenty-six groups.[18] The groups receiving feedback solved their problems more accurately and became more highly motivated to solve future problems than the thirteen control groups. In another study,[19] feedback about both individual performance and the performance of the group as a whole increased the performance of individual members. In still another study, personal feedback of one member to another was shown to improve the efficiency of all.[20] Other research indicates that the amount of feedback is related to the level of performance achieved.[21] For example, training programs involving extensive use of feedback, such as programmed instruction, are generally more effective than conventionally taught training programs without feedback.[22]

The effect of feedback on performance is obvious in the industrial setting as well as in the laboratory. In a study of life insurance agents, Weitz, Antoinetti, and Wallace found that those who received periodic production bulletins and personal letters commenting on their performance improved their average performance, whereas the average performance of a group of agents receiving no feedback actually decreased as compared to a base period.[23] In a series of studies at General Electric, Miller found that increasing the amount of feedback from foremen to workers improved the latter's performance.[24] Hundal as well found that groups of industrial workers who received feedback had higher output than workers who did not.[25]

Several studies indicate that the effects of feedback on performance are influenced by the quality of the feedback. In Miller's General Electric study, the more specific, relevant, and timely the feedback, the greater the positive effects on performance.[26] French also found that feedback was most effective when it was directly relevant to the task,[27] and Trowbridge and Cason, in an early study, found that rapidity of learning was related to the preciseness of the feedback.[28]

Feedback may have effects other than improvements in performance: It may affect the attitudes of recipients. For example, Leavitt and Mueller found that zero feedback was accompanied by low confidence and hostility, whereas free feedback was accompanied by high confidence and friendliness.[29] One study found that as ambiguity decreased with better information, innovative behavior increased and ritualism decreased.[30] In another study, as role expectations became clearer, group satisfaction and effectiveness increased.[31] Kay, Meyer, and French found that under conditions in which the appraisee expected favorable feedback, critical appraisal had a negative effect on attitudes.[32]

Locke and Bryan in two studies found that feedback did not improve performance and that goal setting itself contributed more to performance than knowledge of results.[33] In another study, they found that feedback did improve performance when the subjects used it to establish goals. Locke seems to feel that the feedback of results does not influence performance *unless* the feedback is used as a means of comparing performance with some previously established goal or standard.

DISCUSSION. Locke's point that feedback by itself is only conditionally likely to improve performance is probably true in most situations. However, it is possible that an individual may wish to avoid receiving unfavorable feedback from a superior, even in the absence of a clear performance goal, simply because it is an unpleasant situation. Unlike under experimental conditions, a subordinate usually has definite attitudes and feelings about his boss. Of course, in an MBO program the feedback would always be in relation to a specific goal and therefore could be expected to contribute to performance, given that the subordinate has accepted the performance goal. The research also indicates that feedback will be more helpful to the extent that it is timely, specific, and task relevant. In addition, the research cited shows that feedback can affect attitudes. Under MBO, if the feedback is provided by the superior, it may communicate interest in the subordinate's project or in the subordinate himself. If the feedback is given in a disagreeable manner, it may create resentment and hostility and perhaps contribute to reduced performance.

PARTICIPATION

Participation, or the influence that an individual has on decisions that affect him, can affect performance levels and job satisfaction. For example, in a field study by Lawrence and Smith, two groups of workers who set their own production goals and standards of production had higher production than in the past. In addition, their production increased relative to two control groups in which production goals were not set by the workers themselves but merely discussed by them.[34] Other studies have also shown a positive relationship between participation and the production of rank-and-file workers.[35] Likert reports on two organizations that had substantial productivity increases in one case and substantial cost savings in the other after they shifted over to a more participative approach.[36] One well-controlled study, however, did not show an increase in productivity with an increase in participation.[37]

Participation also results in greater subordinate acceptance of decisions[38] and with proper leadership can result in decisions of high quality.[39] In addition, participation can strengthen agreement among participants,[40] and this mutual understanding may continue past the discussion period itself.[41] Vroom concludes that there is considerable evidence to support the notion that job satisfaction increases with participation.[42]

DISCUSSION. The research on participation and productivity has produced conflicting results. Some studies find a positive relationship, whereas others find none at all. However, there are no studies that suggest that participation will decrease performance. It may be that the key intervening variable is legitimate participation. When an individual does, in fact, have some control over both the means of reaching his goals and the manner in which they are set, this is legitimate participation and higher performance may result. Citing another reason for the conflicting results, Locke[43] has found that several studies showing a positive relationship between participation and performance involved the actual establishment of goals by subordinates; thus, the improvements in performance could be the result of goal setting itself rather than of participation.

Participation is usually related to higher levels of job satisfaction. In addition, it may have benefits other than performance, such as favorably affecting turnover and absenteeism. Participation also seems to be helpful in gaining the subordinate's acceptance of decisions, and it may lead to improved understanding between superiors and subordinates. One better understands what is expected of him if he participates in shaping performance goals. In addition, more participation leads to more discussion, which may in turn lead to better problem identification.

RESEARCH ON ACTUAL MBO PROGRAMS

Only a few studies have been carried out on MBO programs in organizations. Six studies are summarized here. The General Electric research is perhaps the most widely known. The Purex studies attempt to relate hard production criteria to MBO. The Mendleson research examines the superior–subordinate dyad. The English studies and the hospital study present some case studies of the adoption of an MBO program, and the Kentucky studies examine differences in the method of implementing the MBO approach in an organization.

THE GENERAL ELECTRIC STUDIES

In a frequently cited article in the *Harvard Business Review*,[44] Meyer, Kay, and French have summarized the primary findings from a series of studies conducted at the General Electric Company. Their research focused first on a study of alternative methods of performing the appraisal interview and then on the effects of a new MBO program adopted by some managers in the company. Other articles by the authors explain their research results in more detail.[45]

The first research study was carried out after the organization had split the traditional company appraisal interview into two different sessions. The first focused on appraising past performance and taking some action with respect to the individual's salary. The second interview, two weeks later, focused on performance improvement. For the second interview, the authors established an experimental condition that involved having ninety-two subordinates, who had no subordinates of their own, treated in one of two ways. One half of the appraisees were asked to prepare for discussion a set of goals for improving job performance, and the superiors of these appraisees were instructed to allow the latter to exert as much influence as possible on the formulation of the final list of job goals. The other half of the appraisees discussed with their superiors a list of job goals developed by the boss, and over whose final form the superior exerted more influence than the subordinate. All appraisees were studied before and after the performance improvement session and again a few months later with questionnaires and interviews. A number of findings emerged from this study:

1. Greater amounts of criticism and the high threat thus created were associated with more defensive behavior on the part of the appraisees and with lower subsequent performance for those appraisees lower in self-esteem.

2. Appraisees who had more influence in setting goals had more favorable attitudes and achieved a higher percentage of their improvement goals than those with less influence in setting goals. However, appraisees who had been traditionally accustomed to low participation in their relationship with their superior did not perform better under high participation in goal-setting conditions.

3. Goal setting itself was more important than subordinate participation in its effects on improved performance. About 65 per cent of the identified performance deficiencies that were translated into specific work goals resulted in improvements, whereas only about 27 per cent of the identified performance deficiencies that were not translated into specific goals were improved.

These findings were used as guides in developing a program called "Work Planning and Review," which is a form of MBO.

In WPR discussion, the managerial subordinates do not deal in generalities. They consider specific objectively defined work goals and establish the yardstick for measuring performance. These goals stem, of course, from broader departmental objectives and are defined in relation to the individual's position in the departments.[46]

Two groups of appraisees were then studied, one of which used WPR, the other of which operated under a slightly modified version of the traditional performance appraisal method used in the company. Those appraisees operating under the old appraisal method did not change in the areas measured.

The WPR group, by contrast, expressed significantly more favorable attitudes on almost all questionnaire items. Specifically, their attitudes changed in a favorable direction over the year that they participated in the new WPR program with regard to . . . [these areas]:

1. Amount of help the manager was giving them in improving performance on the job.
2. Degree to which the manager was receptive to new ideas and suggestions.
3. Ability of the manager to plan.
4. Extent to which the manager made use of their abilities and experience.
5. Degree to which they felt the goals they were shooting for were what they *should* be.
6. Extent to which they received help from the manager in planning for *future* job opportunities.
7. Value of the performance discussions they had with their managers.[47]

In addition to changes in attitudes, the authors concluded that the members of the WPR group were much more likely to have taken specific actions to improve performance than those operating within a traditional performance appraisal approach.

THE UNIVERSITY OF KENTUCKY STUDIES

A study of the impact of the introduction of an MBO program in two companies was made by Ivancevich, Donnelly, and Lyon.[48] They administered a questionnaire measuring the degree of satisfaction of certain needs, such as self-actualization, autonomy, esteem, social needs, and security—both before and after an MBO program had been introduced. The MBO program was introduced by the personnel department in one organization and in the other by top-level managers. There was more improvement in need-satisfaction scores in the organization in which top-level managers were actively involved in the implementation program, and the most improvement in need satisfaction was among their subordinates in middle management. There appeared to be greater satisfaction in security needs than in the other need categories. In this organization there were also more reviews of performance during the year.

Interviews were also conducted in the study to identify managerial perceptions of the primary problems associated with the new MBO program. In one organization the lower-level managers indicated that they were not actually involved in the MBO program, whereas in the other organization the lower-level managers complained most frequently about the amount of paper work required by the program and about the difficulty of setting goals for their jobs.

THE PUREX STUDIES

Two important studies were reported by Raia, who examined the impact of a program called "Goals and Controls," a variant of MBO.[49] Raia analyzed production records, conducted interviews, and administered questionnaires. The questionnaires were obtained from 112 managers after a goal-setting program was instituted.

By the end of the first year of Goals and Controls, productivity had increased, managers were more aware of the firm's goals, and specific goals had been set in more areas than had been the previous experience. Prior to the program, productivity was decreasing at the rate of .4 per cent per month. After the program was instituted, the trend reversed and was increasing at .3 per cent per month. Raia concluded:

> A contribution of the program in the area of performance appraisal has been quite significant. There was unanimous agreement among the line managers in the department, particularly plant managers, [that] the Goals and Controls had simplified the evaluation of the individuals performance. The statement by the manager who, while being interviewed, remarked that he was now judged by his job performance and not "by the way I comb my hair," is quite meaningful.[50]

Among the other advantages cited were better planning of resource utilization, pinpointing of problem areas, and improved communications and mutual understanding.

There were some problems, however. Raia felt that the company philosophy of the goal-oriented system was not accepted or understood by the individuals using it. Participation was limited, especially at lower levels. Managers believed the program to be a nuisance because of the large amount of paper work involved.

A follow-up study of the same program sheds additional light on the goal-setting program and generally supports the findings of the first study. Raia surveyed the responses of seventy-four managers to the program and analyzed production data.[51] The level of goal attainment increased, and there were continuing increases in productivity in addition to improved managerial planning and control. However, some managers felt that the program was "easy to beat." There seemed to be an overemphasis on production, or measurable, goals. Some of the participants re-evaluated their initial feeling about appraisal and felt that the program did not provide adequate incentives to improve performance. The managers asked: What does it mean to the individual when he fails to meet certain goals? They were not able to link the goal-setting program to the organization's reward system.

THE MENDLESON STUDY

Mendleson undertook to evaluate the relationship between goal-setting techniques and the subordinate's degree of job understanding and rated effectiveness.[52] He constructed an instrument called "The Goal-Setting Index" (GSI) to measure goal-setting behavior. He had a number of specialists or authorities on MBO evaluate the extent to which a set of items described goal-setting behavior and, keeping only those items on which there was satisfactory agreement, he devised the GSI.

He then administered the GSI to twenty-five pairs of superiors and subordinates in eight companies. Basically Mendleson concluded:

1. There was high agreement among the specialists in their description of goal-setting behavior.
2. There was *no* significant relationship between the extent of goal setting in a dyad and the subordinate's understanding of the superior's expectations about the subordinate's job.
3. There was *no* relationship between goal-setting behavior and performance ratings.
4. There was a positive relationship between goal-setting behavior and the subordinate's promotability rating.

These results seem to indicate that goal-setting techniques, by themselves, do not necessarily produce a favorable outcome. Mendleson is quick to point out, however, that his conclusions must be considered in light of the possible limitations of his measurement instrument.

THE ENGLISH CASE STUDIES

MBO has been implemented in many British companies. For example, one management consulting firm has established the MBO approach in more than sixty companies.[53] British experience with MBO has been reported in several case studies.

In one case study, reported by Preston, an MBO plan was introduced into the firm primarily as a better approach for appraising and helping subordinates to develop their abilities rather than as a planning approach.[54] There was some initial resistance from many managers to having responsibility for their subordinates' development. The organization also found that objectives at lower levels could not properly be established unless organizational objectives were communicated along with company policy to the lower levels. The firm reported cash savings in several areas, which they claimed would not have occurred without the MBO program. In addition, there was a feeling that MBO helped management to identify certain problems in the organization and also improved the over-all developmental climate. These results are similar to those reported in case studies of several U.S. firms.[55]

Wickens has reported on a case study of an English company in which the MBO program was introduced by a management consultant but was later discontinued because it did not live up to expectations.[56] Wickens indicates that, although MBO has been successful in many English firms, it has failed in those where it has not been institutionalized. He points out that there are organizational constraints in the successful adoption of the MBO approach, such that it is possible to predict the probable success of an MBO program by a preliminary organizational analysis. In the factory studied by Wickens in which MBO was unsuccessful, a number of factors seemed to be responsible. First, conflicting objectives were established and there were no organizational methods for eliminating such conflicts. Another difficulty was created by a rapidly changing marketing situation, which changed the priority of objectives and problems. In addition, the MBO program was not well integrated with other organizational programs, such as budgeting, production planning, and project schedules. Later, other difficulties arose, such as excessive work loads for top-management personnel, and a reorganization of the organization, which changed the nature of many top-management jobs.

A HOSPITAL STUDY[57]

Sloan and Schrieber introduced in a hospital a program that involved teaching hospital managers how to use the MBO approach by means of formal classroom training and informal discussions with individual managers. Interviews were held with the participants in the program both before and after the training effort took place.

A number of findings emerged from the study. A "critical incidents interview" administered before and after the training indicated that managers were carrying out the performance appraisal and review sessions differently than before the MBO training. They appeared to be more concerned about their subordinates, they improved in their attempts to clarify job objectives and standards of performance, they were more open to suggestions from subordinates, and they seemed to be more perceptive about their own limitations and those of their subordinates.

The participating managers were asked to discuss the advantages and disadvantages of the MBO approach. They said that the major advantage was improved planning and organization of work. The next most frequently mentioned advantage was the clarification of mission, goals, and responsibilities. The most frequently mentioned disadvantage of MBO was the time consumed in carrying out formal requirements of the MBO program and in completing the paper work. The authors feel that managers in a new MBO program probably do spend an excessive amount of time in writing up goals because of their inexperience but that this should diminish with time. However, the posttraining interviews also indicated that most managers felt the MBO program was worth its cost and would be beneficial in the future. They also felt the program would have been even more worth while with greater top-management support.

DISCUSSION OF RESEARCH ON ACTUAL MBO PROGRAMS

The research studies reported here point to some problems in the use of the MBO approach as well as highlight some positive features. One of the positive effects seems to be in *changes in performance and behavior*. Raia described a change in the trend of productivity after the Goals and Controls program was instituted.[58] Prior to MBO, the trend was downward, but productivity began increasing after MBO was introduced. This advance continued during the second year, but the rate decreased.[59] Studies by Raia, and Meyer, Kay, and French reported that those managers working under the MBO program were more likely to "have taken specific actions to improve performance than were those who continued with the traditional performance appraisal approach."[60] Preston's description of an English firm's adoption of MBO supports the view that there are strong potentials for performance changes to occur and that these may well take place.[61]

MBO is also an *aid to managers in performing their jobs*. There is little question, from the studies we have cited thus far, that objectives programs result in better planning. Managers are more aware of higher-management goals, and the awareness of goals is a fundamental prerequisite for planning. In addition, many MBO programs require that methods for attaining goals be established.

A logical by-product of better planning and especially of goal specification is criteria for performance measurement. Most managers involved in these studies report greater satisfaction with the basis for performance measurement. There is also more task-oriented communication between superior and subordinate.

MBO seems to be associated with *positive attitudes toward the work situation*. Managers tend to feel that their abilities are better utilized and that the scope of their authority has broadened. They also have greater feelings of security about their jobs. However, the latter may occur because of increased certainty about the nature of the job, which results from increased superior–subordinate interaction.

As problems with MBO have also been uncovered by these research studies, the *negative effects of MBO* must be compared to its advantages. It must be remembered, however, that these problems may arise because of the way that a particular MBO program is administered rather than because they are inherent in the MBO approach.

Managers report *excessive paper work*. They were generally concerned about the forms and procedures required by MBO and felt that this imposition was important enough to be noted.

The *measurement of performance* is still a difficult problem with MBO. It is easy to set goals in areas where the output can be counted, weighed, or measured in some way. But how does one develop goals in other areas such as the development of personnel or the improvement of relations with subordinates? These problems were noted in Raia's first study and, in the follow-up study, he found that there was a tendency for the goals to be more "production based." This tendency may be simply due to the fact that managers found it too difficult to set goals in other areas.[62] When they did, the goals were not used by their boss for evaluation or reward, and hence they reverted to those goal forms they knew that their boss wanted.

Managers still play the *statistics game*. In his follow-up study, Raia reports that there was a question in some of the respondents' minds about the accuracy of the data reported.[63] This is one of the problems that the objectives approaches are intended to reduce, yet it exists even after the establishment of MBO.

The degree of *stability of the organization* could increase problems of implementing MBO. The Wickens study seems to indicate that organizational instability in terms of reorganization, or rapid changes in technology, or in the marketing situation can be a real threat to the success of an MBO program. He also concluded that the MBO program may fail if it is not adequately integrated into other organizational programs and procedures.[64]

SUMMARY

We have indicated that MBO is used differently by organizations. Some organizations stress the use of MBO as basically a managerial planning approach, whereas most organizations seem to view MBO as primarily a superior method of evaluating performance and conducting performance-appraisal reviews with managers. These two approaches stem from the different emphases given to MBO by Drucker and McGregor, who popularized the MBO concept.

We have also evaluated the research relevant to certain aspects of the MBO approach, such as goal setting, feedback on performance, and participation. This research supports the idea that MBO should result in higher levels of performance than those of management approaches that do not involve the establishment of performance goals, the provision of feedback relevant to performance as it relates to such goals, and subordinate participation in the setting of such goals. The evidence would seem to indicate that the goal-setting process itself would be especially critical to the success of an MBO program, and key factors in setting goals would be their difficulty and specificity or clarity.

The research on organizational MBO programs indicates that the adoption of this approach can improve managerial performance, managerial attitudes, and organizational planning. This research also indicates that MBO programs require considerable time and effort expenditures for successful adoption, and unless they are given adequate support and attention and are well integrated into the organization, they will fail or not live up to expectations. However, research on organizational MBO programs, with the possible exception of the Meyer, Kay, and French studies, has provided few practical guides for actually carrying out the goal-setting and performance-review aspects of the MBO process. In the next chapter, we shall report on a series of studies conducted by the authors on an MBO program in an industrial firm.

NOTES

1. Drucker, P. *The Practice of Management.* New York: Harper, 1954.
2. McGregor, D. *The Human Side of Enterprise.* New York: McGraw-Hill, 1960. McGregor, D. "An Uneasy Look at Performance Appraisal," *Harvard Business Review,* 35 (1957), 89–94.
3. Lewin, K., T. T. Dembo, L. Festinger, and P. S. Sears. "Level of Aspiration," in J. M. Hunt (ed.), *Personality and the Behavior Disorders.* New York: Ronald, 1944, pp. 333–378.
4. McGehee, W. M. "Judgement and Level of Aspiration," *Journal of General Psychology,* 22 (1940), 3–15. Gardner, J. W. "The Use of the Term 'Level of Aspiration,'" *Psychological Review,* 47 (1940), 59–68. Klugman, S. F. "Emotional Stability and Level of Aspiration," *Journal of General Psychology,* 38 (1948), 101–118. Child, I. L., and J. W. Whitney. "Determinants of Level of Aspiration and Evidence from Everyday Life," *Journal of Abnormal and Social Psychology,* 44 (1949), 303–314. Zander, A., and H. Medow.

"Individual and Group Levels of Aspiration," *Human Relations,* **16** (1963), 89–105. Moulton, R. W. "Effects of Success and Failure on Level of Aspiration as Related to Achievement Motives," *Journal of Personality and Social Psychology,* **11** (1965), 399–406. Feather, N. T., and M. R. Saville. "Effects of Amount of Prior Success and Failure on Expectation of Success and Subsequent Task Performance," *Journal of Personality and Social Psychology,* **35** (1967), 226–232.

5. Fryer, F. W. *An Evaluation of Level of Aspiration as a Training Procedure.* Englewood Cliffs, N.J.: Prentice-Hall, 1963.

6. Locke, E. A. "Toward a Theory of Task Motivation and Incentives," *Organizational Behavior and Human Performance,* **3** (1968), 157–189.

7. Stedry, A. C., and E. Kay. "The Effect of Goal Difficulty on Performance: A Field Experiment," *Behavioral Science,* **11** (1966), 459–470.

8. Locke, 1968, op. cit.

9. Locke, E. A. "Performance Goals as Determinants of Level of Performance and Boredom," *Journal of Applied Psychology,* **51** (1967), 120–130.

10. Locke, 1968, op. cit.

11. Locke, 1968, op. cit.

12. Bryan, J. F., and E. A. Locke. "Goal Setting as a Means of Increasing Motivation," *Journal of Applied Psychology,* **51** (1967), 274–277.

13. Locke, 1968, op. cit.

14. Locke, E. A., N. Cartledge, and C. S. Knerr, "Studies of the Relationship Between Satisfaction, Goal-Setting, and Performance," *Organizational Behavior and Human Performance,* **5** (1970), 135–158.

15. Locke, 1968, op. cit.

16. Porter, L. W., and E. E. Lawler III. *Managerial Attitudes and Performance.* Homewood, Ill.: Irwin, 1968. Atkinson, J. W., and N. T. Feather. *A Theory of Achievement Motivation.* New York: Wiley, 1966.

17. Stedry, A. C. *Budget Control and Cost Behavior.* Englewood Cliffs, N.J.: Prentice-Hall, 1960.

18. Pryer, M. W., and B. M. Bass. "Some Effects of Feedback on Behavior in Groups," *Technical Report 13,* Contract N70NR 35609. Baton Rouge, La.: Louisiana State University, 1957.

19. Zajonc, R. B. "The Effects of Feedback and Group Task Difficulty on Individual and Group Performance," *Technical Report 15,* Contract NONR 1224 (34). Ann Arbor, Mich.: University of Michigan, 1961.

20. Smith, E. E., and S. S. Knight. "Effects of Feedback on Insight and Problem Solving Efficiency in Training Groups," *Journal of Applied Psychology,* **43** (1959), 209–211.

21. Taylor, A., and C. E. Noble. "Acquisition and Extinction Phenomena in Human Trial and Error Learning Under Different Schedules of Reinforcing Feedback," *Perceptual and Motor Skills,* **15** (1962), 31–44. Chinn, R. C., and E. A. Alluisi. "Effect of Three Kinds of Knowledge of Results Information on Three Measures of Vigilance Performance," *Perceptual and Motor Skills,* **3** (1964), 901–912. Hammer, C. H., and S. Ringel. "The Effect of the Amount of Information Provided and Feedback of Results on Decision Making Efficiency," *Human Factors,* **7** (1965), 513–519.

22. Schramm, W. *The Research on Programmed Instruction: An Annotated Bibliography.* U.S. Dept. of H.E.W. Washington, D.C.: G.P.O., 1964.

23. Weitz, J. A., J. Antoinetti, and S. R. Wallace. "The Effect of Home Office Contact on Sales Performance," *Personnel Psychology,* **7** (1954), 381–384.
24. Miller, L. *The Use of Knowledge of Results in Improving the Performance of Hourly Operators.* General Electric Company, Behavioral Research Service, 1965.
25. Hundal, P. S. "Knowledge of Performance as an Incentive in Repetitive Industrial Work," *Journal of Applied Psychology,* **53** (1969), 224–226.
26. Miller, 1965, op. cit.
27. French, E. G. "Effects of the Interaction of Feedback and Motivation on Task Performance," *American Psychologist,* **11** (1956), 395 (abstract).
28. Trowbridge, M. H., and H. Cason. "An Experimental Study of Thorndike's Theory of Learning," *Journal of Genetic Psychology,* **7** (1932), 245–260.
29. Leavitt, H. J., and R. A. Mueller. "Some Effects of Feedback on Communication," *Human Relations,* **4** (1951), 401–410.
30. Hamblin, R. L., and J. A. Wiggins. "Ambiguity and the Rate of Social Adaptation," *Technical Report 1,* Contract ONR 811 (16). St. Louis: Washington University, 1959.
31. Smith, E. E. "The Effects of Clear and Unclear Role Expectations on Group Productivity and Defensiveness," *Journal of Abnormal and Social Psychology,* **55** (1957), 213–217.
32. Kay, E., H. H. Meyer, and J. R. P. French, Jr. "The Effect of Threat in a Performance Appraisal Interview," *Journal of Applied Psychology,* **49** 1965, 311–317.
33. Locke, 1968, op. cit.
34. Lawrence, L. C., and P. C. Smith. "Group Decision and Employee Participation," *Journal of Applied Psychology,* **39** (1955), 334–337.
35. Coch, L., and J. R. P. French, Jr. "Overcoming Resistance to Change," *Human Relations* **1** (1948), 512–532. Whyte, W. F. *Money and Motivation.* New York: Harper, 1955.
36. Likert, R. *New Patterns of Management.* New York: McGraw-Hill, 1961.
37. Morse, N. C., and E. Reimer. "The Experimental Change of a Major Organizational Variable," *Journal of Abnormal and Social Psychology,* **52** (1956), 120–129.
38. Maier, N. R. *Problem Solving Discussions and Conferences.* New York: McGraw-Hill, 1963.
39. Maier, N. R. "The Quality of Group Decisions as Influenced by the Discussion Leader," *Human Relations,* **3** (1950), 155–174. Maier, N. R. F., and L. R. Hoffman. "Using Trained 'Developmental' Discussion Leaders to Improve Further The Quality of Group Discussions," *Journal of Applied Psychology,* **44** (1960), 247–251.
40. Hare, A. P. "Small Group Discussions with Participatory and Supervisory Leadership," *Journal of Abnormal and Social Psychology,* **48** (1953), 273–275. McKeachie, W. J. "Individual Conformity to Attitudes of Classroom Groups," *Journal of Abnormal and Social Psychology,* **49** (1954), 282–289.
41. Bovard, E. W., Jr. "Social Norms and the Individual," *Journal of Abnormal and Social Psychology,* **43** (1948), 62–69. Cohen, E. "Stimulus Conditions as Factors in Social Change," *American Psychologists,* **11** (1956), 407.
42. Vroom, V. *Motivation in Management.* New York: American Foundation for Management Research, 1965.

43. Locke, 1968, op. cit.
44. Meyer, H. H., E. Kay, and J. R. P. French. "Split Roles in Performance Appraisal," *Harvard Business Review,* **43** (1965), 123–129.
45. Kay, Meyer, and French, 1965, op. cit. French, J. R. P., Jr., E. Kay, and H. H. Meyer, "Participation and the Appraisal System," *Human Relations,* **19** (1966), 3–19.
46. Meyer, Kay, and French, 1965, op. cit.
47. Meyer, Kay, and French, 1965, op. cit.
48. Ivancevich, J. M., J. H. Donnelly, and H. L. Lyon. "A Study of the Impact of Management by Objectives on Perceived Need Satisfaction," *Personnel Psychology,* **23** (1970), 139–151.
49. Raia, A. P. "Goal Setting and Self Control," *Journal of Management Studies,* **2** (1965), 34–53.
50. Raia, 1965, op. cit.
51. Raia, A. P. "A Second Look at Goals and Controls," *California Management Review,* **8** (1966), 49–58.
52. Mendleson, J. L. "Managerial Goal Setting: An Exploration into Meaning and Measurement." Unpublished doctoral dissertation, Michigan State University, 1967.
53. Wickens, J. D. "Management by Objectives: An Appraisal," *Journal of Management Studies,* **5** (1968), 365–379.
54. Preston, S. J. "J. Stone's Management by Objectives," *Personnel* (London) **1** (1968), 22–25.
55. Wikstrom, W. S. "Managing by—and with—Objectives" (Studies in Personnel Policy No. 212), *National Industrial Conference Board* (1968), 1–21.
56. Wickens, 1968, op. cit.
57. Sloan, S., and D. E. Schrieber. *Hospital Management . . . An Evaluation.,* Monograph No. 4. Bureau of Business Research and Service, Graduate School of Business. Madison, Wis.: The University of Wisconsin, 1971.
58. Raia, 1965, op. cit.
59. Raia, 1966, op. cit.
60. Raia, 1965, 1966, op cit. Meyer, Kay, and French, 1965, op. cit.
61. Preston, 1968, op. cit.
62. Raia, 1965, op. cit.
63. Raia, 1966, op. cit.
64. Wickens, 1968, op. cit.

2

AN INTENSIVE STUDY OF MBO

Any organization considering MBO must be aware of the factors that influence its success or failure. Before MBO is introduced, answers to certain questions should be obtained. What should top management do to make the MBO program effective? How should the program be introduced to management? Is training needed, and if so, what kind? What should managers be asked to do under this program? Do other elements or programs have to be changed because of the introduction of MBO?

Each individual manager using MBO also has certain questions to answer. Should the goals that are set be easy or difficult? Should priorities be set for goals? How many goals should be set? Who should set the goals? Me? My subordinate? Both of us?

The conduct of the review process also raises questions. Should I leave my subordinate alone after the goals are set, or should I talk to him frequently about his progress? How much should I praise or criticize him

21

in these intermediate review sessions? How much pressure should I put on him to accomplish his goals? Another very important question facing each manager is whether he should carry out the MBO process differently for each of his subordinates. Are difficult goals good for Tom but bad for Harry? Should I leave Jerry alone after goals are established, or should I review his performance as much as I do Bill's?

To seek answers to such questions, the authors conducted an intensive research study on MBO in a large national manufacturing firm with a reputation for being progressive and innovative.

THE FIRST MBO PROGRAM

MBO was instituted on relatively short notice at the initiative of a recently appointed vice-president of personnel. A reporting form was developed, the program explained to top management, and instructions sent to the rest of the managers. There was a short implementation effort. Basically most managers were left to their own devices in their application of MBO.

The managers carried out the goal-setting and review processes in many different ways, a fact that turned out to be advantageous. First, it was possible to examine the relationships between the results and the different methods of conducting the goal-setting and review processes. Second, because of the variability of subordinates' personalities, attitudes, and job assignments, we were able to examine how certain personality and situational characteristics of the subordinate affected the relationship between the results obtained and various methods and characteristics of the MBO process.

The research was conducted in two phases. The first was an interview study, in which a sample of fifty managers, drawn from various levels and functional areas in the company, were asked a set of detailed questions about their experience with the MBO process. The objective of this approach was to obtain general reactions to the new MBO program and to identify the critical aspects of the MBO process in order to study them in more depth in a second phase, a questionnaire study.

I. THE INTERVIEW STUDY*

Each of the fifty managers in the sample was interviewed by one of the authors (the schedule of questions is in Appendix A, at the end of the book). Usable data were collected from forty-eight individuals. Each manager

---

* This section is based on an article by the authors entitled "Managerial Reaction to Management by Objectives," *Academy of Management Journal*, **11** (1968), 415–426. By permission of the publisher.

interviewed was asked to enumerate and explain the purposes of the program, the advantages of using the MBO approach, the primary problems involved in implementing and carrying out an MBO program, and the suggestions he had for the improvement of the program. These areas were probed in some detail in the interview. Table 1 shows the number of managers at various organizational levels who participated in this study.

TABLE 1   NUMBER OF MANAGERS
AND THEIR LEVELS

Management Level	Number
Vice-President	6
Director	12
Middle management	20
Lower management	10

FINDINGS: MANAGERIAL REACTIONS TO MBO

PHILOSOPHY, RATIONALE, AND PURPOSE OF THE PROGRAM.   During the interview, each manager was asked the following questions. What are the purposes of the program as you see them? What is the rationale for this approach? Table 2 presents a summary of the responses.

TABLE 2   PHILOSOPHY AND RATIONALE OF THE OBJECTIVES APPROACH

	Rationale	n^*	%
1.	Link evaluation to performance	17	35.4
2.	Aid manager in planning	12	25.0
3.	Motivate managers	11	22.9
4.	Increase boss–subordinate interaction and feedback	11	22.9
5.	Develop management potential	8	16.6
6.	Link company objectives to department objectives	8	16.6
7.	Managers know what their job is	6	12.5
8.	Give management information about what's going on at lower levels	4	8.3
9.	Management club to pressure performance	3	6.25
10.	No mention	7	14.5

* n = 48 managers.

The purposes cited most frequently tend to parallel those stated in the company manual that introduced MBO. The largest percentage (35 per cent) felt that an objectives program was intended to link the individual's evaluation to his actual performance rather than to personal characteristics. About 25 per cent considered the approach useful as a planning aid. Increased feedback and the positive motivational effect of the objectives approach was mentioned by more than 22 per cent of the respondents.

The data suggest little general agreement among managers about the underlying philosophy and rationale of the program. Only one item, "the attempt to relate evaluation to performance," was noted by more than 30 per cent of the respondents. It could be that those items cited most frequently, that is, evaluation, feedback, planning, and motivation, were the respondents' verbalization of what they remembered of the organization's MBO manual. It appears therefore that the attempts to introduce and initiate the program did not substantially affect the previous attitudes and knowledge of the individual managers about MBO.

ADVANTAGES. The managers were asked the advantages of the objectives program; these are summarized in Table 3. By far, the major advantage was that one was more likely to "know what is expected of him

TABLE 3   ADVANTAGES OF MBO

	Advantage	n^*	%
1.	I know what is expected of me	28	58.6
2.	Forces planning and setting target dates	20	41.6
3.	Forces boss–subordinate feedback and communication	15	31.2
4.	Increases awareness of company goals	9	18.7
5.	Documents goals relating evaluation to performance	8	16.6
6.	Focuses on self-improvement	7	14.5
7.	I know where I stand	6	12.5
8.	Coordinates activity toward company objectives	6	12.5
9.	Subtle pressure and motivation to perform better	5	10.4
10.	Improves performance if used	4	8.3
11.	Only a general help	3	6.2
12.	No advantages mentioned	5	10.4

* n = 48 managers.

by his boss." Over 58 per cent noted this advantage. One marketing executive noted:

> Now we can focus our evaluation on what people do, rather than what they are. This is the best thing we have for evaluating the performance of our men. And it has a substantial motivational effect. These goals set up a challenge for them. I have seen changes in men's work habits after I began to use this approach. I have been able to watch improvements occur in some of my men.

An engineer felt that

> while I did not have much to say in what the final determination of my goals were, at least I knew what my boss wanted and I knew what to do. I think this motivated me to work harder, or at least to work on those things that I knew were important to him. I also knew whether or not I achieved targets set for me.

The next item cited most frequently (41 per cent) was that the program forced more planning, specification of projects, and setting target dates. As one of the managers indicated,

> There is a kind of discipline involved in this program. I had to sit down and think about what I am going to be doing next year. I need to spell out what kind of resources are required and when I expect a particular project to be accomplished. This is a great help to me in determining what priorities should exist. Of course, it is an advantage to have these priorities verified by your boss.

Several managers (31.2 per cent) felt that it forced bosses to interact with their subordinates, providing more communication and feedback. One of the respondents, who had recently joined the firm, thought it to be

> a fantastic idea to have a voice along with your boss in setting individual goals. Not only do you get a chance to put your two cents' worth in but it gives your boss the benefit of the individual's thinking. I thought it was a psychological lift. I like the fact that they asked me what I thought my goal levels should be. I think the chance to sit down with your boss is important.

Another manager said,

> I like the fact that I sit down with my boss to set these objectives. Every time I sit down and talk with him I can't help but learn more about what he expects of me. Anything that does that is a help.

The advantages found here are fairly consistent with those one would have expected and with those found earlier by Raia.[1] The most frequently cited advantages that Raia noted were (1) planning, (2) pinpointing problem areas, (3) objective performance measure, and (4) improved communications. It seems reasonable to conclude that objectives-oriented programs increase certainty about job requirements, result in a more comfortable feeling about the kind of criteria used in evaluation, and create a situation that ostensibly forces superiors to communicate with subordinates.

PROBLEMS ENCOUNTERED. A number of managers (37.5 per cent) indicated no problems with the objectives approach. The major problem, cited by 43 per cent of the managers, was compliance with the formal procedural requirements—the processes of completing forms, updating changes, and providing other information to the personnel unit. Raia and other investigators also found this a major irritant and dubbed it the "paper-work problem."[2]

Some (20.8 per cent) felt that the objectives approach was not used to its full potential in the organization. One of the respondents said:

> I am not sure that many managers know how to use and develop objectives and goals. Everyone seems to think in terms of "target dates." Some jobs just don't lend themselves to that kind of goal. We need to recognize that different kinds of goals and objectives might be required for different functions, different jobs, and maybe even different managerial levels. Yet if you look at these review sheets all the goals look the same—a project designation and a target date. And besides, the self-improvement goals really seem to be just an appendage and not an integral part of the process.

TABLE 4   PROBLEMS AND DISADVANTAGES ASSOCIATED WITH MBO

Problem	n*	%
1. Excessive formal requirements	21	43.7
2. Not used to full potential	10	20.8
3. Need to consider different goals for different jobs and levels	7	14.5
4. Never get good feedback	7	14.5
5. I was never really involved in the program	7	14.5
6. It is undesirable to commit oneself to goals formally	5	10.5
7. Lack of information about personal characteristics	2	4.2
8. No real problems	18	37.5

* n = 48 managers.

In general, with the exception of the problems noted above, the problems and disadvantages tended to be fairly well distributed across the range of items listed in Table 4.

SUGGESTIONS FOR PROGRAM CHANGES. Additional information about problem areas developed when the managers were asked: How would you improve the program? Table 5 shows the suggestions and the percentage of managers making them. The major responses to this question point to a lack of top-management support, use, and reinforcement. With the exception of item 4, the suggestions focus on the use of the program by superiors.

The second item in Table 5 bears repetition. Over 40 per cent of the managers indicated that after their goals had been set, their time had been pre-empted by higher levels of management and they were made to work on another project. In most cases, this change was not noted formally on the review forms. Although most agreed that their immediate superior took this into consideration in evaluation, some expressed concern that if their boss left and a new man came in, "He would find that I did not achieve any of the objectives on the form; consequently, my performance might be evaluated lower than it was." Several felt somewhat anxious and threatened because they had to commit themselves on paper to goals that might well change because of demands upon them over which they had little control.

TABLE 5   SUGGESTIONS FOR IMPROVING THE OBJECTIVES PROGRAM

	Suggestions	n*	%
1.	Ensure review and feedback	24	50.0
2.	Develop a way to update goals so that changes can be noted	20	41.6
3.	Use by top management so that *their* goals are known at lower levels	19	39.5
4.	Include "personal" evaluations in addition to goals	16	33.3
5.	Top-management support for the program	15	31.2
6.	Increase the understanding of the program and how to set goals	12	24.9
7.	Include "normal job requirements"	10	20.8
8.	Due dates of program are incompatible with unit planning and control cycles	7	14.5
9.	Ensure "real" participation and involvement in goal setting	5	10.4
10.	Others	11	22.9

* $n = 48$ managers.

FINDINGS: STRUCTURAL FACTORS AND INFLUENCES IN THE MBO PROCESS*

From the interview, some analysis was made of the relationship between superior and subordinate influence in the choice of goals and certain structural factors. These factors were (1) the organizational unit, (2) the organizational level, and (3) the goal-setting process.

In the interview, respondents were asked to describe the manner in which the goal-setting process occurred with their boss. From these reports categories of influence were developed in the goal-setting process.

INFLUENCE MEASURE. The degree of influence over performance goals was determined by asking managers the question: Who had the most influence over the performance goals that finally ended up on your Work-Planning and Review form? Responses were evaluated and grouped into one of three categories:

> Category 1.   Boss has the most influence.
> Category 2.   Mutual influence of boss and subordinate.
> Category 3.   Subordinate has most influence.

These were used to construct an influence index within each analytical class.

SUBORDINATE INFLUENCE AND THE ORGANIZATIONAL UNIT. The influence index was constructed for each major functional area of the firm. Executives were interviewed from the marketing, finance, manufacturing, and engineering divisions of the organization. (Other units are not included in this analysis because of the small numbers in these divisions.) Figure 2–1 shows the number of executives and the influence index derived for each area from the interview data. As would be expected, the degree of influence is different for each major functional area. Data from the interview indicate that influence over performance goals was highest in the marketing division, which includes activities such as sales, distribution, and product service. Because most of the interactions are external, crossing the boundary of the organization, they may be less susceptible to control by the organization, and perhaps less predictable. Thus, higher management levels would be more dependent upon those in the field for the assessment of realistic performance levels as well as for the determination of appropriate strategies.

The next-highest influence index was in the finance and administration area, the functions of which, in this organization, were both rapidly

---

*   This section is based on an article by the authors entitled "Some Structural Factors Related to Goal Influence in the Management by Objectives Process," *MSU Business Topics,* 17 (1969), 45–50. By permission of the publisher.

FIGURE 2–1   PERCEIVED INFLUENCE INDEX IN EACH
              FUNCTIONAL AREA

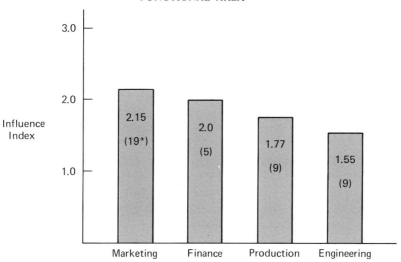

*Indicates number of managers interviewed
who provided usable data.

changing and highly technical. Different types of demands were often made on this unit by other parts of the organization, in addition to which the organization was moving toward an improved computer information system to be located in this division. Under these conditions, one might expect that subordinate managers below the top level would have a great deal of influence over the goals, as they often have technical skills or expertise in specific fields that is greater than that held by their superiors—although the superiors may have broader knowledge and skills.

The manufacturing division ranked next in the degree of influence. Influence levels should be lower here because activity is largely dependent on other units in the organization. Factors such as sales forecasts, production procedures, schedules, and methods are some determinants of behavior within this unit. It follows, therefore, that the individual in this unit is likely to be more influenced by the system than he is able to affect it.

Finally, the engineering division had the lowest influence index. One might have expected members of this unit to have reported the greatest degree of influence over their performance goals. However, closer scrutiny of the activities of this unit uncovered the fact that engineers work on applied projects that are generally product changes or adaptations. These are usually specified by higher-level management and invariably last for long periods. Obviously, when an engineer is committed to one of these, he has little to say about what activities and projects he will work on; this is determined for him.

We can speculate about the differences. Any student of organization would be remiss if he failed to point out that these differences may be due to the climate induced by the managerial style of key executives in each department. But, although there is no question that this factor may have a substantial impact, the importance of structural and technical considerations cannot be overlooked.

SUBORDINATE INFLUENCE AND THE ORGANIZATIONAL LEVEL. In another phase of the research, we examined differences in influence at various organizational levels. Influence indices, shown in Figure 2-2, were constructed from the interview data for each organizational level. The general relationship between level and influence was as expected. Those at the highest organizational level reported having the greatest influence over their performance goals. The influence index decreased for the next two lower levels. And,

FIGURE 2–2   PERCEIVED INFLUENCE INDEX AS REPORTED BY MANAGERS AT EACH ORGANIZATIONAL LEVEL

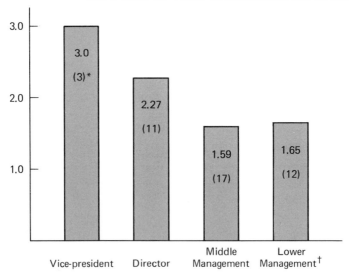

*Indicates number of managers interviewed who provided usable data.

†Includes two lower levels, combined here for ease of analysis.

although it is true that those at the bottom level had a slightly higher index than those at the immediately higher level, the general trend of influence still tended to decrease as organizational level decreased.

The results are generally consistent with the structure of most organizations; that is, the manager's discretion area is smaller at lower organizational levels. There is other supporting evidence that indicates that this holds true even in objectives programs. Raia reported that the number of supervisors actively involved in goal setting decreased at succeedingly lower organizational levels.[3] The same problem of participation and influence was examined here and the findings are consistent with those of Raia. Thus, the traditional concept of organizational structure and the decreasing discretion at lower levels of the organization impose a practical limitation on the nature and the degree of involvement and influence that can result from an objectives program.

SUBORDINATE INFLUENCE AND THE GOAL-SETTING PROCESS. Some of our most important research dealt with the specific manner in which the goals were set. We wanted to find out how superiors and subordinates determined, negotiated, and agreed upon the goal levels and activities to serve as performance targets. Each manager was asked: How was the goal setting carried out? What happened first? Second? Next? Figure 2–3, derived from the interview discussions, shows the number of managers who reported different types of goal-setting processes and the general influence index for each process. These processes are described below.

Process 1. The process with the highest levels of mutual involvement was designated as process 1. Generally, the superior would first hold a department meeting during which the unit goals and projects for the coming operating period were discussed. The subordinate would then, using the information from this general meeting, prepare a set of personal goals. At the same time, the boss would independently prepare a set of goals and targets for the subordinate. Later they would meet to discuss these and arrive at some mutual agreement on the subordinate's goals. Twenty-eight per cent of the managers reported using this goal-setting process.

Process 2. In process 2 the boss was somewhat less involved. Goal setting usually began with an informational meeting in which the general departmental and organizational objectives were discussed. Later the subordinate prepared a set of goals and target dates, which he gave to his boss. Rather than preparing a set of goals for the subordinate, the boss edited and altered those prepared by the subordinate. When a meeting was held to discuss the goals, the basis for discussion was the subordinate's edited and revised goal statement. Approximately 21 per cent of the managers used this type of approach.

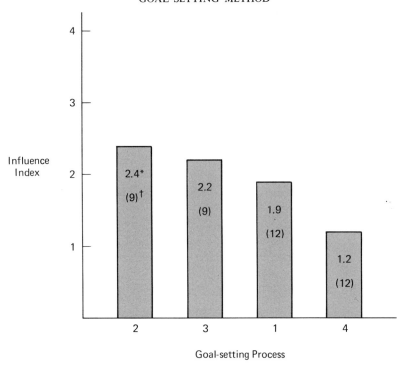

FIGURE 2–3   INFLUENCE INDEX AS A FUNCTION OF
GOAL-SETTING METHOD

Influence Index

Goal-setting Process

*Lower scores indicate lower influence.

†Figures in parentheses indicate number of
managers reporting.

Process 3. Still another variant in the goal-setting process was reported by some 21 per cent of the managers. First, the boss called a general meeting to discuss departmental objectives. From this, subordinates prepared individual goal statements, which they sent to the boss. However, contrary to processes 1 and 2, these goal statements were accepted without any meeting or discussion. The subordinate did not have the opportunity to determine whether or not the goals were acceptable to his boss. He could only assume that they were so by the superior's silence.

Process 4. This was the most "boss-centered" process. The subordinate was simply informed about the objectives program. The boss and the subordinate met, at which time the subordinate was given a set of goals that the boss had prepared. The subordinate had little to say about the goals and the target dates set for them.

THE GOAL-SETTING PROCESS AND PERCEIVED INFLUENCE. As one would expect from the various processes described above, the subordinate's perception of his influence on performance goals varied. The influence index that was constructed for each process is shown in Figure 2–3. The lowest index (1.2) is for process 4, in which the goals were prepared by the superior. Process 1, in which there were the highest levels of mutual involvement and preparation, had the next-lowest index (1.9). Although there is much more subordinate involvement in process 1 than in process 4, the superior is still seen as having slightly more influence than the subordinate. In processes 2 and 3, the influence index was 2.4 and 2.2, respectively. In both, the subordinate felt that he had greater influence than his boss over the goals set. This certainly seems reasonable. In types 1 and 4, there is more superior involvement and physical presence. Meetings in types 2 and 3 tend to be more subordinate dominated; apparently the boss is less involved.

The perceived influence over goals may be related to the presence of the superior: The more he is there, the more his influence is felt. This is consistent with cultural perceptions of the superior–subordinate relationship in organizations; that is, the boss should have more to say about subordinate goals than the subordinate does. This feeling may be heightened when the superior is physically present and involved in the goal-setting process.

II. THE QUESTIONNAIRE STUDY

One hundred fifty (150) managers from all levels were selected to receive mail questionnaires. Some 135 managers responded and 129 questionnaires contained usable data. The fifty-item questionnaire (reproduced in Appendix A) was based on the results of the interview study, the examination of relevant research on goal setting, and the provision of feedback on performance.

FOCUS OF STUDY

The items on the questionnaire focused on the goal-setting process; the review process; attitudes toward the boss, the company, and the MBO program; job characteristics; subordinate characteristics; and work accomplishments during the year that the MBO program was put into operation. Many of the items were combined into scales. For example, responses to questions about the applicability of MBO to the subordinate manager's job, how well the subordinate liked the MBO program, and how helpful the MBO program had been to the subordinate in performing his job duties were combined into one measure of subordinate reaction to the MBO program.

The questionnaire was directed toward discovering the manager's *perceptions* of how the MBO effort was used, because it is the perceived, and not necessarily the actual, behavior of the boss that influences subordinate behavior and attitudes.

CHARACTERISTICS OF GOALS. The goal characteristics measured were difficulty of goals, general clarity of goals, number of goals set, amount of subordinate influence in establishing goals, and whether priorities were established for goals.

CHARACTERISTICS OF THE REVIEW PROCESS. The dimensions of the review process examined were frequency of review, amount of praise versus criticism given, and degree of superior stress on the importance of goal accomplishment.

CHARACTERISTICS OF THE BOSS–SUBORDINATE RELATIONSHIP. The various aspects of the relationship between boss and subordinate that were analyzed were the amount of time the boss spent on MBO, the perceived managerial support for the program, the perceived amount of participation, the degree of satisfaction with the boss, and the amount of boss involvement in the subordinate's job.

CRITERIA OF PROGRAM SUCCESS. The criteria of program success consisted of scales constructed from data reported by the managers themselves in the questionnaire survey. These included the increase in effort over previous years, orientation toward the WPR program (positive or negative), success in accomplishing assigned performance and self-improvement goals, and changes in relations with the superior (positive or negative).

PERSONALITY AND SITUATIONAL FACTORS. Managers were grouped into approximately equal "high" and "low" groups on a number of situational and personality variables. The goal, review, and superior–subordinate relationship dimensions were then correlated with the criteria within each of these high and low groups.

The situational moderators, consisting of scales constructed from the questionnaire responses, were job satisfaction, respondent's perception of the relationship between performance and reward, job interest, control over means of goal achievement, and perceived amount of help and support from the superior.

Scores used on the personality dimensions were determined by responses to the Ghiselli Self-Description Inventory, with the exception of "need for structure," which was constructed from questionnaire responses. The Ghiselli personality factors were self-assurance, maturity, self-perceived intelligence, decisiveness, and perceived supervisory ability.

The results of this analysis will not be presented in detail, as they are available in a number of technical articles, some of which are included in Appendix B. Instead, these personality and situational characteristics will be discussed generally in the concluding section of this chapter.

FINDINGS: THE GOAL-SETTING PROCESS*

GENERAL FINDINGS. With regard to the relationship between the different ways in which goals were established and the four criteria considered as program success measures, we found the following statistically significant relations:

1. More difficult goals were associated with subordinate managers' being more positive toward the MBO program.
2. As goals increased in perceived clarity, importance, and relevance, subordinate managers
   a. were more positive toward the MBO program.
   b. reported that they had improved their relations with their boss over previous periods.
3. When priorities were established for goals, subordinate managers
   a. were more positive toward the MBO program.
   b. improved their relations with the boss over previous periods.
4. The amount of subordinate influence in establishing goals was not significantly related to any of the four measures of MBO success.
5. The number of goals established was not significantly related to any of the four measures of MBO success.

These findings would indicate that, as goals became more clear, important, and relevant, managers were more positive toward the MBO approach and toward their boss who was involved in the establishment of such goals. More difficult goals also were associated with more positive feelings toward the program. At first glance, it would seem that, as goals were more difficult, managers would be less favorably oriented toward the program. But perhaps having more difficult goals leads the subordinate to conclude that the company and the boss are taking the program seriously.

ADDITIONAL FINDINGS ON SUBORDINATE INFLUENCE IN SETTING GOALS. As indicated previously, subordinate influence in the goal-setting process was not related to reactions to the program or to the various measures of MBO

---

* This section is based on an article by the authors entitled "Goal Characteristics and Personality Factors in a Management by Objectives Program," *Administrative Science Quarterly*, **15** (1970), 295–305. By permission of the publisher.

program success that were used. However, in the General Electric studies discussed in Chapter 1, it was found that influence in setting goals was related to performance primarily in subordinates accustomed to day-to-day participation in job activities.[4] If the subordinate was not used to participation, he did not do well with high participation in setting goals. In our study we related influence in the establishment of goals to performance in those subordinates for whom job participation was usual. The results obtained were similar to those obtained in the General Electric studies. There was a *small* positive relationship between the degree of subordinate influence in setting goals and effort expenditures and goal success for subordinates used to participation but not for subordinates unused to participation.*

OTHER FINDINGS ON THE GOAL-SETTING PROCESS. The goal-setting characteristics were also significantly related to some other factors. For example, greater goal clarity was associated with a feeling that the boss had spent more time on the MBO program and therefore with a feeling of satisfaction with the boss. Increased subordinate influence on goal setting was associated with higher perceived general influence on the everyday decision-making activities of the job. When the boss established priorities for goals, the subordinate saw the boss as more supportive and helpful.

FINDINGS: THE REVIEW PROCESS†

GENERAL FINDINGS. Differences in the subordinate manager's perception of the review process were significantly related to differences in the measure of success of the MBO program in the following ways:

1. Higher feedback frequencies were associated with
   a. higher satisfaction with the MBO program.
   b. higher reported goal accomplishment.
   c. improved relations with the boss compared to previous time periods.

---

* For the group who typically had lower participation on the job ($n = 54$), influence over performance goals correlated $r = -.03$ to effort increase and $r = -.16$ to goal success. For the group who typically had higher participation on the job ($n = 66$), subordinate influence over performance goals correlated $r = .21$ for effort increase and $r = .12$ for goal success. Although only the r of .21 is statistically significant at the .05 level for these n's, the others are in the direction obtained with a similar breakdown in the General Electric studies.

† This section is based on an article by the authors entitled "The Relationship of Characteristics of the Review Process as Moderated by Personality and Situational Factors to the Success of the 'Management by Objectives' Approach," *Proceedings, Academy of Management*, 1969, 139–143. By permission of the publisher.

2. Higher amounts of praise and lower amounts of criticism were associated with
   a. greater reported goal success.
   b. higher goal levels being set in the next goal-setting period.
3. Stronger perceptions that the boss was quite concerned with goal accomplishment were associated with more positive feelings about the MBO program.

These data suggest that the more frequent review may result in more positive attitudes toward MBO, better boss relations, and higher goal accomplishment. This of course does not necessarily mean that the frequency of performance review should be unlimited, as this may be viewed as too close a supervision.

The results indicated a relationship between the amount of praise and accomplishment. Actually we might expect that praise was more frequent when there was greater goal success and that goal success in one period would be related to the establishment of even higher goals in the next period, because the level of aspiration and expectations generally rises after successful performance. We would also expect that subordinate managers would have more positive feelings about a company's MBO program if the subordinate's boss seemed to take the program seriously.

OTHER FINDINGS ON THE REVIEW PROCESS. As the frequency of review and the feeling that the boss would be concerned about goal failure increased, subordinate managers reported more goal clarity, higher perceived amounts of organizational support for the MBO program, a perception of greater boss time expenditures on the MBO program, more satisfaction with the boss, and more frequent perceptions that the boss was helpful and concerned about the subordinate. These findings also suggest that the emphasis placed by the boss on the MBO program, which is demonstrated by the way that he carries it out, is quite consistently related to subordinates' perceptions of the program.

FINDINGS: SUPERIOR–SUBORDINATE RELATIONSHIPS*

Some of the various aspects of the boss–subordinate relationship were related to the end-result variables. The following significant relationships emerged from this analysis:

---

* This section is based on an article by the authors entitled "Some Factors Affecting the Success of 'Management by Objectives,'" *Journal of Management Studies,* 7 (1970), 209–223. By permission of the publisher.

1. The more time the boss spent on MBO,
   a. the more satisfied the subordinate was with MBO.
   b. the greater the perceived goal success.
   c. the more improved the relationship with the boss.
   d. the lower the perceived effort increase.
2. The more perceived organizational support for MBO, the more satisfied the subordinate with MBO.
3. The greater the amount of perceived usual participation, the more improved the relationship with the boss.
4. The greater the satisfaction with the boss,
   a. the more satisfied the subordinate with MBO.
   b. the greater the perceived goal success.
   c. the more improved the relationship with the boss.
5. Higher levels of boss involvement in the subordinate's job were associated with improved relationships with the boss.

These findings suggest that the interpersonal relationship with the boss is an important factor in the reaction of an individual to MBO. In general, the more positively the subordinate views the boss, the more likely he is to have positive attitudes toward MBO. Note too that the amount of effort that the boss is thought to have put into MBO is related to a number of the end-result variables. This only emphasizes the significance of the superior–subordinate relationship to the success of a new program.

FINDINGS: FACTORS RELATED TO HOW THE SUPERIOR CARRIES OUT THE MBO PROCESS*

The sample of managers was used to identify superior–subordinate pairs for which research data were available. Then personal characteristics and various situational factors for the superior were statistically related to how that superior carried out the MBO process, as reported by his subordinates. A number of findings emerged from this analysis.

It was found that the manner in which the boss of the superior carried out the MBO process with *him* was related to how the superior carried out the MBO process with his subordinates. For example,

1. Clearer goals for the superior were associated with clearer goals for the subordinate.

---

* This section is based on an article by the authors, with D. Cintron, entitled "Factors Related to How Superiors Set Goals and Review Performance for Their Subordinates," *Proceedings*, *American Psychological Association*, 1971, pp. 497–498. Reprinted by permission of the American Psychological Association.

2. Higher amounts of participation on the part of the superior in setting goals was related to greater subordinate participation in setting goals.
3. More frequent review of the superior's performance by his boss was related to the superior's more frequent review of the subordinates' performance.
4. The establishment of priorities among the superior's goals was associated with the establishment of priorities among the goals for the subordinates of that superior.

Another analysis indicated that a number of personal characteristics and perceptions of the superior were related to how effectively he carried out the MBO process with his subordinates. In this analysis, it was assumed, on the basis of previous findings, that superiors who set clear and difficult goals and carried out the review process frequently were more effective at carrying out the MBO process. The findings from this analysis indicated that higher goal clarity, goal difficulty, and frequency of performance review were associated with

1. Higher amounts of perceived organizational support for the MBO program by the superior.
2. More job satisfaction for the superior.
3. Perceptions by the superior that his boss would be very concerned with any goal failure on his part.
4. Higher amounts of decisiveness as compared to cautiousness for the superior.
5. Higher amounts of self-assurance for the superior.

Finally, the data also indicated that higher amounts of subordinate influence in goal setting were related to higher ratings of competence for the subordinate and that subordinates who were more similar to their superiors in measured personality characteristics were more similar to their superiors in the way that they carried out the MBO process.

These findings seem to indicate that subordinates imitate their superiors to a certain extent in carrying out the goal-setting and performance review processes with the men who report to them. The data here also seemed to indicate that superiors carry out the MBO process more effectively when they perceive organizational support and concern for the MBO program at higher levels and when they themselves have the traits of decisiveness and self-assurance that have been associated with higher management effectiveness in other studies.[5]

CONCLUSIONS

We have described here some of the major findings from an intensive study of MBO. These findings lead us to a set of conclusions that may be of some value to others now using the MBO approach or considering its use for the future. All too often, managers at *all* levels and in *all* functions are prodded to use MBO. Because influence over goals is often assumed to be an important factor in the MBO process, when we introduce an MBO program we often have to change the expectations of individuals as to the amount of involvement and participation they can expect to have. Otherwise, incompatibilities among personality, organization, and influence are liable to create dissatisfactions.

THE RESULTS OF THE QUESTIONNAIRE STUDY

Perhaps the largest number of findings was developed from the analysis of the questionnaire. As a result of these data, it was concluded that the manner in which the MBO process is implemented has substantial effects and that personality characteristics and different job situations do make a difference.

THE GOAL-SETTING PROCESS. The research clearly indicates that the clarity and the relevance of goals established in MBO are important determinants of the response to it. Clear and relevant goals were related to all favorable reactions and to no unfavorable ones. The same holds true for the establishment of priorities among goals: the relationships are all positive. The research suggests, however, that clear goals may be more important to some managerial groups than to others. For example, to obtain higher effort levels from managers, clear goals may be especially important for those with lower job interest and for important-decision makers. Clear goals are also related to higher levels of satisfaction with the superior and to a subordinate perception that the objectives program is important. Results also indicate that goal clarity may be to some extent a function of other aspects of the objectives process. Objectives probably become clearer to subordinate managers as the amount of time spent on the program by the superior increases. This may be especially true when the number of feedback and review sessions is greater. The more feedback, the clearer the goals may become. Thus, in general, the data indicate that for all types of subordinates, the goals established should focus on important areas of departmental and personal need, they should be clearly stated in terms of the results expected, and the relative importance of the various goals should be pointed out.

Difficult goals, on the other hand, are not always associated with positive outcomes. For example, although difficult goals led to higher effort expenditures among managers high in self-assurance, they were related to lower effort expenditures for those managers with less confidence in themselves. In addition, more difficult goals were related to higher increases in effort among managers who felt that there was a relationship between performance and rewards. Thus, it would appear that difficult goals stimulate some managers and discourage others. Similar results were obtained when the managers were grouped into high and low levels of maturity. Difficult goals had a positive relationship with effort increases among mature managers and a negative relationship among the less mature and experienced managers. In general then, it is important for the superior to consider the characteristics of his individual subordinates before establishing the level of their regular performance and self-improvement goals. In general, the data seem to indicate that difficult goals are more positively received by the more confident, more mature, more career-oriented manager.

Having large numbers of goals was not associated with any negative results. In fact, setting a large number of goals resulted in greater effort expenditures among those subordinates who worked for supportive and helpful bosses. Perhaps there is more acceptance of difficult work assignments from a highly supportive boss.

Having priorities for goals was also related to a number of what might be considered favorable effects, such as a more positive feeling about the MBO program and improved relations with one's superior. This was especially true for those managers who were relatively lower in self-perceived intelligence, who were cautious in their decision making, who did not associate higher performance with rewards, and who had a high need for structure.

Finally, the degree of subordinate influence in the goal-setting process does not seem to be an important factor in the perceived success of the objectives program. Subordinate participation in setting goals did not result in higher levels of perceived goal success or of effort expenditures (except in one case), nor in more favorable attitudes toward the superior. However, subordinate influence did have a small positive relationship to effort expenditures, goal success, and improvements in relations with the boss, when the subordinates had typically been allowed to participate in decisions with their bosses. Subordinate influence over performance goals had a small negative relationship to goal success and to relations with the boss, when there was a typical pattern of low subordinate influence or participation in the job decisions. This would seem to indicate that having managers in an MBO program force their subordinates to participate in setting goals will not result in better responses to the MBO program, unless such participation is part of the superior's typical management style. However, even with subordinates used to participation, influence in establishing goals is not important when compared to such factors as the difficulty and clarity of goals. As indicated in Chapter 1, Locke has pointed out that, in earlier studies, participation involved actual goal setting by subordinates, and therefore the motivational effects of participation where goal setting is really used might be expected to be slight.[6]

THE REVIEW PROCESS.   The research suggests that feedback frequency is an important determinant of the success of MBO. Virtually all the relationships between feedback frequency and the criteria variables were positive. For example, higher feedback frequency was related to more favorable attitudes toward the program, higher goal success, improvement in the relationship with the superior, a perception that the organization supports the WPR program, a feeling of supportiveness and interest from one's superior, and satisfaction with the superior. Our data also indicated that feedback frequency seems especially important to managers low in self-assurance, cautious in decision making, and with jobs involving frequent change.

It therefore seems desirable for those managers who use the MBO approach to schedule and carry out frequent performance review sessions with each subordinate. The "end of the period" review seems less than adequate. Most managers in MBO programs are probably not conducting enough review sessions, and an effort should be made to determine why this is true. A personal time analysis may identify activities that could be eliminated, or delegated, so as to give the manager more time for managing. This could result in increased interaction with the subordinate, during which review feedback and coaching can take place.

If feedback is limited because managers view the process as being uncomfortable, the obvious approach is to increase the amount of training. Role playing, as well as other methods, could improve managerial interpersonal communication abilities.

The data indicate that praising managers for good performance and criticizing them for bad was generally related to a positive outcome in terms of our criteria, although this depended somewhat on the characteristics of the managers. Those, for example, who saw little relationship between performance and advancement were apparently not influenced too much by praise or criticism. The data also indicate that the superior should make the subordinate aware that goal accomplishment is important to him and that negative sanctions may be imposed if the goals are not met. This seems more important for managers who are cautious and for those who are less satisfied in their present organizational situation.

THE SUPERIOR–SUBORDINATE RELATIONSHIP.   The subordinate's reaction to the managerial style of his superior is demonstrably a function of the individual subordinate's personality and the situation. High-initiative managers tend to be more positively oriented toward the boss's efforts to become more involved with them, either in a general sense or by increased levels of participation.

Participation, in a general sense, had essentially positive effects, and, for the most part, they were stronger on high-initiative managers or on those with greater needs for certainty or structure. It is important to note that, although, as mentioned earlier, the level of specific goal influence in MBO was not generally related to the result variables, here a more general type of participation or general influence in one's work was related to our outcome variables. The practical applications of this finding are obvious. To have any impact, participation in goal setting must be part of a more general overall managerial style consistent with mutual goal setting. The subordinate must be given the opportunity to participate meaningfully in more than setting goals.

THE SUPERIOR'S CHARACTERISTICS.   There is some imitation of superiors by subordinates with respect to the former's method of setting goals and reviewing performance. This would indicate that it is important for higher-level executives to realize that they serve as models of the MBO process and therefore should take great care that they carry out this process in an effective manner. In addition, the research indicated that MBO will be more effective if the superiors communicate to their subordinates that the MBO program is of importance to them and that they will be concerned if good results are not achieved. Finally, there was support in the data for the belief that one can expect MBO to be carried out more effectively by those managers in the organization who are already better managers.

RESULTS OF THE INTERVIEW STUDY

Results from the interview study have implications for the implementation of an MBO program. The study indicated that managers see some positive aspects of MBO but may not be aware of all the benefits unless significant efforts are made to acquaint them with such advantages. Managers are more likely to be enthusiastic about a new MBO program if they see real benefits for themselves from it. This lack of awareness of the advantages of the MBO approach may be characteristic of top-level management as well as of lower-level managers. The second most common perceived problem for the MBO program was that it was not being used to its full potential. In addition, the study indicated that, if the paper-work problem were reduced, managers might perceive of MBO as having no problems: Most managers either indicated no problems at all with the approach (37.5 per cent) or indicated only a paper-work problem (43 per cent). The MBO program certainly does not need to be excessively formal.

The importance of higher-level management's commitment to the MBO program was shown by the fact that the most common suggestions for improving the program were that more review of performance be provided, as it relates to goals, that goals be updated when conditions change, and that higher levels participate more so that higher-level goals are known to lower-level personnel. It is certainly probable that only when all levels of management reinforce the subordinate's participation in the MBO program and use the system themselves will significant benefits result from this approach.

There is evidence in the organization studied that many superiors were not supporting the MBO program. As one manager said,

> I have never been asked by my boss whether or not I used this system. I don't know whether he really cares about it.

Another indicated to one of the authors:

> We ought to go at this full blast or not at all. I haven't had to answer to my boss for the fact that I haven't set objectives this year. We need some indication that management is really behind us. I can't really be sure, but I think the program is beneficial.

Results indicate that managers view the review aspect of MBO as being of significant importance. The biggest advantage of MBO, as they saw it, was that it provided them with information on performance expectations, thus reducing role ambiguity. The most important reason for its use as perceived by the managers was to link evaluation to performance; yet only 12 per cent of those interviewed felt they "really knew where they stood." The most common suggestion of the managers for improving the MBO program was that review and feedback be made a consistent part of the program. These findings indicated that the review process was not being carried out adequately in the organization studied, even though managers were quite concerned about how their performance was reviewed. This suggests that provisions must be built into the MBO program for ensuring that performance review is at least adequate.

Our data suggest that there are certain kinds of organizational constraints that seem to be related to the degree of influence over goals. Factors such as the organizational level and functional field, for instance, were found to be related to influence levels. Level and functional field are less susceptible to change and alteration by management than other organizational variables. In addition, some organizational assignments and the structure of some jobs are difficult to alter. When this is the case, the influence must be treated in terms of the interpersonal relationship between the boss and the subordinate. Our data would suggest handling goal setting in such a way as to increase the perceptions of influence.

It is obvious from all this that the main problems with MBO lie not in the basic characteristics of the approach itself but in the way that it is used by individual organizations and managers within those organizations. Most of the reasons cited for a reduction in the effectiveness of an MBO program are management practices that would limit the effectiveness of any new program. It also seems to be true that problems involving planning, motivation, and appraisal do not fade away with the mere adoption of the MBO approach. How the program is implemented and carried out is critical.

SUMMARY

These data show the importance of organizational commitment to MBO. Managers must feel that the MBO program is important, that the company is serious about it. It is necessary that organizational goals become clear, as goal setting at all lower levels is more difficult and perhaps even impossible without clear goals that can be fashioned into the departmental or individual goals. Managers must have time and resources so that they can utilize MBO. In addition, the time and energy requirements of the program should not be excessive.

An important finding of this research is that MBO affects different managers in different ways. The results obtained indicate that in many respects MBO should be tailored to the individual and his position rather than being presented as a single, defined approach for all managers. Some of the findings indicate in what ways MBO should be tailored to fit certain types of managers.

NOTES

1. Raia, A. P. "Goal Setting and Self Control," *Journal of Management Studies,* **2** (1965), 34–53.
2. Raia, 1965, op. cit.
3. Raia, A. P. "Management by Objectives in Theory and Practice," *Southern Journal of Business,* (1968), 11–20.

4. French, J. R. P., Jr., E. Kay, and H. H. Meyer. "Participation and the Appraisal System," *Human Relations,* **19** (1966), 3–19.
5. Wickert, F., and D. McFarland (eds.). *Measuring Executive Effectiveness.* New York: Appleton, 1970.
6. Locke, E. A. "Toward a Theory of Task Motivation and Incentives," *Organizational Behavior and Human Performance,* **3** (1968), 157–189.

3

IMPLEMENTATION OF MBO

Chapters 1 and 2 dealt extensively with research underlying the MBO process. From the emphasis on research, methodology, and theoretical considerations in Chapter 2, we now turn to the practical problems of implementing an MBO program.

SOME ORGANIZATIONAL CONSIDERATIONS

Some broad-policy problems must be resolved before MBO can effectively be implemented. For example, MBO must be integrated with the other components of the formal structure, such as the subsystems of budgeting, man-power planning, appraisal, and development. If such compatibility does not exist, several problems may arise in the future, as in the case study of an English firm cited earlier, in which there was no integration of the subsystems with the MBO program.[1]

There must be some consideration given to the manner in which goal setting will take place. Some advocates of MBO would argue for a fairly formalized and scheduled series of meetings between superiors and subordinates to ensure that the conditions for effective goal setting are present. Others argue that goal setting should be the responsibility of the superior and the subordinate and that how it is done should be left to them.

Such mechanistic questions as the following: What kind of appraisal forms are to be used? How are they to be used? Should the interview between the boss and the subordinate be the primary vehicle for the evaluation, or should the evaluation be recorded on some form? must be resolved. More important, however is the answer to the question: What should be the content of the interview? Meyer, Kay, and French suggested the separation of discussions about performance from salary considerations.[2] Also in an English case study, the separation of performance review from the establishment of merit pay increases seemed to result in fewer problems.[3] However, when performance and compensation are discussed separately, it becomes very difficult for the individual to link performance with salary and promotion, thus potentially reducing the effectiveness of salary as an incentive. Previous research has shown that managers who perceive a relationship between performance and the reward system perform at a higher level.[4] Thus, if management prefers to link incentives and performance, goal accomplishment and salary can be considered at the same time.

Frequency of performance appraisal is an important issue. There should be at least one required annual performance review. This should be supplemented with intermittent reviews. Our research suggests that the frequency of performance review is related to many positive managerial attitudes and to higher performance.

Once an individual's performance has been evaluated and discussed extensively with him, how much of the information gleaned from this process needs to be submitted to higher levels of management, recorded in his personnel file, and made generally available to others in the organization? What information should be provided to the subordinate? Such information may have substantial impact on an individual's future in the organization and must be handled with care.

In the event that a manager lacks the necessary skills to set goals or appraise performance, will some sort of training effort be available? Or should the development of these skills be the responsibility of one's immediate superior? If there are deficiencies, especially in goal setting, the whole MBO process breaks down. Because this skill is so critical to the success of MBO, its development should be provided for either by training or intensive coaching.

Once major goal areas have been set at the top-management level, the freedom of action that lower and middle managers have in choosing their own goals should be interfered with only when necessary. However, if the original goals have been formally recorded, a change in them should be made formally. Otherwise, at the end of the appraisal period, goals that are no longer relevant will still be listed on a form, and a manager may well become uneasy. In later periods when the form on which the original goals were recorded is examined by others, a manager might be evaluated as a failure because he did not achieve those particular goals.

The answers to all these questions will serve as a guide in the implementation of MBO and are problems that top management must contend with before attempting to implement any type of formal MBO system.

MANAGERIAL RESISTANCE TO MBO

Individuals may not be fully receptive to a formal MBO program. Although most managers no doubt feel that the philosophy of MBO is an important one—one that they believe that they use—a formal program will cause some problems and encounter some managerial resistance to change. Some of the problems are those discussed in Chapter 2. In addition, there were also some subtle indications of resistance to MBO in the interview study described in that chapter, although most of these were encountered in such a way that they were difficult to document.

TIME EXPENDITURES

"I've always managed this way. Why do I have to spend time in training? Why do I need to write these goals? My people know what is expected." Comments such as these indicate that some managers feel that the determination of objectives takes an unreasonable amount of time. There is little question that the development and statement of objectives and subsequent programs of action will take a great deal of a manager's effort and time. When a formal MBO program is used, the manager must communicate the goals and objectives of the organization. These must be developed and prepared in such a way that they can be clearly stated to his subordinates, as well as to his superiors. This means that a manager will be forced to spend time, which may be in very short supply for him, to prepare his objectives and to assist his subordinates in preparing their objectives in such a way as to facilitate communication.

SUBORDINATE DEFICIENCIES

Another problem is that some managers may not believe their subordinates capable of using MBO because they lack the adequate decision discretion necessary to participate effectively in MBO or are not competent enough to make the proper decisions. However, what is more likely to be the case is that managers who resist MBO are either underestimating the competence of their subordinates or rationalizing their own unwillingness to allow additional subordinate involvement and participation.

EROSION OF AUTHORITY

Because of subordinate participation in setting objectives, a superior may feel that he is losing some control, that his authority is being eroded. This concern probably arises from a lack of understanding of the relationship among participation, discretion, and decision parameters. To participate means that an individual has influence on the decision. If subordinates do, in fact, participate in decision making, their input should be valued and used when appropriate. Essentially, the subordinate must have some discretion to act in the area in which he is participating. (Discretion can come either from a general policy or from the delegation of responsibility and authority by a superior.) However, in some cases, it may not be appropriate for the subordinate to influence the decision, for instance, parameters such as budget limitations imposed by top management may make certain decisions nonnegotiable. What is of utmost importance in this case is that the subordinate know what these nonnegotiable areas are. In this way, there is better understanding between the superior and the subordinate as to which areas the subordinate may participate in, and which areas he cannot participate in.

LACK OF PLANNING ABILITY

MBO forces managers, especially at the top levels, to look ahead to the future. In two organizations studied, the authors found a great deal of reluctance on the part of certain high-level but very disorganized managers to look ahead and establish specific objectives for their organizational units. As MBO forces an analysis of the future, managers who are reluctant to do this may resist MBO.

STATUS OF THE GROUP PROPOSING THE PROGRAM

In the University of Kentucky studies cited earlier, a new MBO program was more successful when it was initiated by the top-management group than when it was initiated by the personnel department.[5] Certainly perceptions of the initiator will influence acceptance. Initiators of any new program who are perceived by others to be of low status, low competence, untrustworthy, or who are disliked because of past behavior will have difficulty in gaining acceptance for their suggested programs.

MBO AS A "CLUB"

Some managers feel that MBO is a club used by the organization or superiors to compel them to perform at higher levels than they are able to. In an unpublished study, Stein, who interviewed several hundred managers participating in an MBO program[6] found that a manager may feel that he is forced to commit himself to unrealistic or undesirable goals simply because he is unable to argue effectively against such goals.

THE MBO CYCLE AND WORK CYCLE

Other planning and work cycles may not be compatible with the formal MBO cycle. For example, sometimes there will be scheduled evaluations whose dates may not coincide with the planning and control cycles of the various units in the organization. The end of the fiscal year may be the time specified for the annual performance evaluation under MBO, but some units may be operating on a calendar-year basis. This means that different goal-setting and evaluation cycles would be appropriate for them. Different cycles must be taken into account.

DISLIKE OF THE PERFORMANCE REVIEW REQUIREMENTS

When MBO is implemented, the intended review and feedback may not take place as needed or required. Many managers make the mistaken assumption that when they interact with their subordinates, the subordinates receive feedback about their performance. Such is not the case. When goals are set in MBO, they represent a statement of the superior's expectation of the subordinate's work and provide the subordinate with guidelines delineating his responsibilities and activities. Having these stated in "objective form" leads the individual to expect some feedback. When performance feedback is not forthcoming, particularly with respect to goals set, he may be somewhat upset, frustrated, and concerned with how he is being evaluated. Therefore, if MBO does create an expectancy for feedback, we must ensure that it occurs *and that the subordinate perceives it as feedback*. Some managers dislike the face-to-face discussion of performance with their subordinates. One manager interviewed by one of the authors indicated that he hated to review performance with his subordinates. This activity caused him considerable discomfort and was decidedly unpleasant to him. He did not like the MBO program, preferring instead the old performance review program, which involved using groups of superiors from several levels to review the performance of engineering personnel. Obviously he liked the group evaluations because he could share responsibility for his judgments and suggestions.

PAPER-WORK PROBLEMS

In our research we have found paper work to be an irritant for a certain number of managers. There is no doubt that more work is involved for the MBO manager. Goals and evaluations should be documented, which means additional forms. Becoming bogged down in paper work does reduce time for other managerial activities. However, it is possible that the paper-work syndrome is simply the easiest rationalization for failing to use MBO. Furthermore, it has been our experience that this is only an initial response. Later, managers are more willing to use the MBO system and prepare a goal statement, if the program is implemented with the true support and assistance of top management.

IMPLEMENTATION OF MBO

To implement MBO, an integrated, well-designed program should be developed that will enhance the chances of MBO's acceptance by managers and will contribute to its effectiveness. Like any new program, MBO must be fully understood; managers must know why and how it works. In addition, they must both be motivated to use it and have the ability to implement it.

The implementation effort should take place in at least three stages: learning, implementation, and follow-up.

THE LEARNING PHASE

There are some important skills that managers must develop before they can use MBO effectively. In addition, there are various types of information that will facilitate its use. The following areas are of utmost importance and must be covered in the "learning phase."

WHAT MBO IS. Managers must know as much as possible about MBO and its value. Emphasis must be placed on the planning aspect as well as on the goal-setting and appraisal dimensions of MBO. In the learning phase, theory and practice should be tied together. Managers should examine the value of participation, feedback, and goal-setting and learn how these relate to performance and satisfaction on the job. The details of goal setting in the organization must be discussed, in addition to the sequencing of goal-setting and evaluation activities. These can be tied in with other organizational activities, such as budgeting, performance evaluation, salary, and promotional review.

THE MANAGEMENT PHILOSOPHY AND MBO. Managers must know how MBO fits into the general philosophical framework of management in the organization. This is especially important because MBO and top-management philosophy must be consistent. Simply verbalizing support for MBO is not enough to ensure its implementation. However, the process of thinking through the relationship between MBO and management philosophy, especially by top management, forces the kind of commitment and decisions that must be made prior to implementing MBO. Managers, especially those at the higher levels, are also forced to become aware of the problems that will be encountered in the future and, more importantly, to think of specific ways to resolve these problems.

GOAL SETTING. Managers should know in what ways the general objectives of the organization can be broken down into meaningful objectives for lower-level units. Translation of general objectives into operational terms for lower levels must be part of the training effort. For example, objectives can be viewed as means–end chains to show that the goals and objectives of one unit are the means used by a higher-level unit to achieve its objectives. An understanding of means–end chains is thus helpful in the determination of lower-unit objectives.

Certain training techniques, such as the problem-solving methods of Kepner and Tregoe, and Maier, may be very helpful in goal setting.[7] After all, goals may be viewed as a type of problem to be solved, and the ability to define well the problems to be solved can facilitate the development of various solution strategies.

Managers must know the difference between objectively and subjectively measured goals. This becomes especially acute in the appraisal process and in the development of performance measures, as the nature of the performance standards will have an impact on managerial performance. Because grave misunderstanding can result from using poorly developed and understood performance standards as a basis for evaluation, managers must know the difficulties in the development of effective evaluation criteria.

APPRAISAL. Part of the training should focus on appraisal. Role playing can make managers more aware of the difficulty of conducting appraisal interviews. For example, defensiveness resulting from criticism can be brought out more directly when experienced in role playing. Using the appropriate training methods, managers can learn techniques to reduce defensiveness in the appraisal process.

SUMMARY. Once these subject areas have been covered in detail, managers are in a better position to know the relationship between MBO and their job. This understanding, developed through active participation and involvement in the learning phase, will facilitate the use of MBO on the job.

An external consultant might be extremely helpful in this phase of the introduction. The practicing manager probably has neither the time nor the inclination to develop an understanding and explanation of the underlying theory of MBO; he is more concerned with practice. The consultant can bring to bear experiences and skills in training managers to use MBO, and can make certain that the manager is exposed to both the positive and negative aspects of MBO.

Training for MBO, however, may cause some of the resistance to it. As many managers may believe that they use it already or that another approach is more effective for them, training is directed at changing a managerial style. This means that the training process must allow the participants the opportunity to practice the skills, assess them, and ultimately arrive at their own judgment regarding the advantages of MBO. Thus, extensive time during the program should be devoted not only to the discussion of how MBO works but to the opportunity to understand the benefits derived from it as well as the typical problems encountered with it.

Essentially, the learning process described so far will increase knowledge of MBO and develop basic skills, but it cannot guarantee that

MBO will be used effectively on the job. Thus, the learning phase represents only the first step. Because implementation occurs on the job, the organization's environment must be supportive of the MBO process. That is, the ideas developed in the learning phase must be consistent with existing norms that underlie the superior–subordinate relationship and the managerial philosophy that generally permeates the organization. These, and the decisions and policies resulting from them, will have the most substantial effect on whether managers use MBO effectively and their attitudes toward it. If managers find that the reward system pays off for behavior other than that recommended in the objectives process, MBO will achieve only secondary status. If it is not part of the ongoing system of the organization, it will be shoved aside and viewed as a useless appendage to the manager's job. He will view it as excessive paper work, to be completed only because the personnel department requires it. If this is his perception, MBO will be relatively valueless to him.

THE IMPLEMENTATION OF MBO

As stated above, the developmental experiences described in the learning phase will probably expose the manager adequately to the theory of MBO and provide some basic practice in its requisite skills, but the key to successful implementation is the use of MBO by top management. Verbal support is not enough to get managers at lower levels to use the system. Because they are unlikely to use it unless their superiors use it, it may be necessary to implement MBO in a relatively structured fashion.

THE STATEMENT OF GOALS. The most fundamental problem to be resolved is the definition of the organization's objectives. These must be defined as clearly as possible and then stated both as desired results and as the general plans and programs to achieve them. If not, individuals at lower levels will be unable to determine how they can contribute to the goals. The determination of organizational objectives will be one of the most valuable contributions of MBO, as it forces top management to review and assess the objectives of the firm and state them in an operational fashion.

Goals cannot be stated in simple, general terms. For instance, it is not enough to state that we want to be the "leader in the field." An operational definition of what leadership in the field means must be developed. Is it measured by increased market penetration? If so, how much? Is it the rate of new product introduction for the following year? Broad philosophical statements of abstract ends may be relatively meaningless to lower-level managers—one reason it is important that the organizational goals be the subject of intense concern at the top level.

THE CASCADING PROCESS. The responsibility, of course, for developing these goals is top management's—probably the chief executive's. He may do it in conjunction with the board of directors or a group of vice-presidents at the level below him. Once the goals and general plans have been developed, they must be clearly communicated to the next-lower levels. This can be done by a series of cascading meetings. The cascading process is nothing more than a set of meetings between the superior and his work group to deal with the objectives of the boss.

First, the corporate executive officer determines his objectives and general program. Then he meets with all his immediate subordinates, including staff and operating executives in charge of major divisions. At this meeting he defines his objectives and plans for the group. Essentially, this is a statement of what he believes to be the major activities and goal areas for the following year. The purpose of this meeting, especially for the subordinate, is informational.

At the meeting, subordinates should be given the opportunity to increase their understanding of how the chief executive sees the direction, goals, and plans of the company through a free flow of information about objectives. Negotiable and nonnegotiable areas and plans should also be discussed, as these will become operating constraints for lower-level managers. At this meeting, there is only slight emphasis on the specific goals and objectives of the subordinates.

From the information received at this group meeting, each manager should develop a plan of action, goals, and appropriate performance measures for each relevant organizational objective in his own unit or division. Then, in a private meeting with the chief executive officer, each manager undertakes to make an assessment of his own goals and what he will do to achieve them. When these goals and specific plans of action are agreed upon, precise goals and ways of achieving them will exist for two levels of management.

Once an executive at the second level knows what his objectives are, he schedules a meeting with his operating and staff personnel. At this meeting, he makes known to that group the goals and action plans that he has agreed to with his boss. This group meeting is essentially an informational one, at which subordinates should be encouraged to ask questions and engage in discussion that will help them understand the kinds of commitments that have been made to the higher level. The subordinate can then make a more accurate assessment of his discretion areas. He will know those areas in which he can make decisions, in addition to those that are nonnegotiable, non-decision-making areas for him.

After this group meeting, each third-level executive individually prepares a set of action plans and objectives for himself and his unit, and then meets individually with his superior. At this time the superior and the subordinate agree upon the goals, activities, and criteria for assessment of success.

When some consensus has been reached and the executive has his set of goals, he should then schedule a meeting with his subordinates and the process described above continues. This cascading process should proceed to the lowest level of the organization feasible. At each succeedingly lower level, the range of individual discretion will, of course, become less and less, as an individual at the lower level will have more of his activities specified for him. This may mean that for the lowest operating managerial level, the meetings are essentially communicational in nature. The subordinate may be given a fairly well-developed set of operating measures and action plans that he must implement. The nature of the organizational beast is such that these managers must operate within tighter organizational constraints than managers at higher levels.

Some difficult problems must be resolved in this cascading process, or else there will be a breakdown in MBO. The first one is timing. For the cascading process to occur effectively, the meetings between superiors and subordinates should be fairly tightly scheduled; otherwise, the goal setting process may extend over a long period of time. Weeks or months could be spent in refining the general organizational goals to meaningful operational components for managers of lower levels. We therefore suggest that a specific period be devoted toward goal setting—perhaps the two-week period immediately following the final budget determination for the following fiscal year. If managers know that a particular time is scheduled for goal setting, they can schedule other commitments appropriately so as to be available to engage in that activity.

Another problem is the amount of individual time involved in the determination of objectives and action plans. We have already noted that one general complaint voiced by managers is that MBO takes what they regard as an inordinate amount of time. Perhaps they are already burdened with too many activities. It is our contention, however, that MBO is a way to be an effective manager. Therefore, managers must either find the time or make it.

Another important problem is the possibility of a break in the goal-setting chain. If, at any level, a manager fails to set goals, those at lower levels cannot effectively use MBO. This is perhaps the primary reason that goal setting should be done during a specific time. Managers can then be held accountable for setting goals. As a matter of fact, one goal that might be set for all managers by their superiors is to have goals set for subordinate groups. Their success in this area can be verified later in the evaluation of performance. Managers can be asked to bring with them to the evaluation discussion the goal statements developed earlier with their subordinates.

THE EVALUATION OF PERFORMANCE. Our research suggests that managers feel that they do not receive adequate performance review and feedback.[8] On the other hand, most managers would argue that they supply subordinates with adequate information on performance. They say, for example: "I hold a group meeting every Monday morning to discuss the past week's results," or "I sit with my subordinates at least once a week and talk with them about their progress." This is not the kind of review and feedback activity necessary to make MBO effective because subordinates generally do not regard these activities as feedback. Group meetings are usually situations in which there is limited specific information given to any one individual about his performance. (If such specific information were given in a group meeting, it would probably arouse intense defensiveness of those in attendance.) General meetings are usually viewed by subordinates as situations in which the manager, seeking solutions, presents his own problems to his work group. The review and feedback process should be more personalized—one in which the managers and subordinates operate on one-to-one basis.

In most organizations at least one annual performance review is required. The reason, normally, is to provide data on promotability and appraisal for personnel records, in addition to the desire to convey performance review information to individuals. Our data suggest that one meeting a year is not frequent enough; more frequent feedback is necessary for positive results of MBO.[9] Therefore, intermediate review meetings should be scheduled.

More meetings will undoubtedly take more of the manager's time. But we would argue that this is his job, his responsibility. These intermediate review sessions might be held on a quarterly basis, or perhaps more frequently or randomly through the period. They would no doubt be more effective if they took place at the end of some major activity. For instance, if one of the major components of a subordinate's objectives is to complete a subtask at the end of a specified time, say three months, the intermediate review session should be held at the end of the three-month period. It should be clearly stated that the intermediate review session is a review session, at which progress can be reviewed, problems solved, and some assistance given to the subordinate in working toward his goals. These intermediate sessions will provide an opportunity for both positive feedback, such as praise and recognition, and negative feedback.

It is our contention that there must be some formal mechanism to ensure that appraisal occurs. For example, the personnel department can develop some sort of monitoring system, through which the department operates as a support unit for facilitating the appraisal process rather than requiring it to meet formal requirements. Otherwise, managers may feel that reviews are conducted primarily for providing information to the personnel department rather than for the appraisal of subordinates.

THE FOLLOW-UP

After the MBO program has been formally implemented and is in operation, some assessment should be made of how it is used by managers. Undoubtedly, problems will occur that need to be discovered and resolved.

There should be constant ongoing discussion with managers about difficulties with forms, format, and other specific problems of goal setting or appraisal. There is also the need for a well-conceived, formal follow-up evaluation. This formal evaluation—in which there is an examination of the goal-setting process, generally recurring problems with MBO, suggested changes, and the manager's reaction to the program—should probably occur about eighteen months after the program has been formally instituted.

A follow-up may be helpful in uncovering some important problems. For instance, it may help to pinpoint whether the goal-setting and evaluation processes have broken down in any of the departments. If so, action can be taken to reinforce goal setting, and pressure can be brought to bear on those managers who are not using the MBO process. If this is not desirable, a fairly extensive general educational effort can be undertaken to make these managers aware of the value of MBO.

The follow-up will uncover cases in which MBO is incompatible with other systems. For instance, where there are discrepancies between the compensation program and MBO, they will be highlighted in the follow-up study. Constant monitoring of MBO is important because of the benefits to be derived from altering the program to fit the needs of the managers.

It is our feeling that it will take approximately three to five years to build an MBO process into an organization such that it becomes part of the managerial style and philosophy. Follow-up evaluation of the process is necessary to facilitate this integration, as it is only then that the process can be tailored to the needs of the company and the philosophy of the management.

THE USE OF CONSULTANTS.   The external consultant will be of importance in performing this auditing function. In this capacity, he may investigate areas in which the program, once implemented, needs to be changed and improved.

It is important to stress here that this external agent should be primarily used in the training and in the auditing phase. During the implementation stage, he should act only as a critical observer. The program must be implemented by the managers themselves.

SOME RESEARCH ON IMPLEMENTATION

The suggested method of implementation discussed in the first part of this chapter grew out of our experiences with evaluating and altering the MBO effort in one firm. On the basis of the problems uncovered in our evaluation, we developed the strategy previously suggested. In this section, the results of the change program are analyzed.

THE EARLIER MBO SYSTEM

In an earlier publication and in Chapter 2, it was noted that the MBO program was

> instituted at the initiative and the authority of a new vice-president of personnel. He found, on joining the company, that the appraisal system was essentially based on "personality traits and characteristics." The Personnel Department began developing manuals and procedures necessary for the change to an objectives oriented appraisal system. These were prepared and distributed. Meetings were held with the top-management group in the company to discuss the use and rationale underlying the objectives approach. They were instructed to implement it in their own units. Needless to say, the degree of implementation and management support varied within different departments.[10]

The reactions of managers to this program were analyzed from interviews conducted with a sample of 50 of the company's managers and from a questionnaire administered to 150 managers. Although there were some fairly positive reactions, the following problems were apparent from the data:

1. There was generally a lack of awareness of the rationale and value of the WPR (MBO) approach.
2. There was insufficient mutual goal setting.
3. There was not enough time spent on periodically reviewing performance during the year.
4. There was a feeling that the WPR program was too rigid and formal.

5. There was inadequate knowledge about top management goals.
6. Superiors and subordinates lacked understanding of how to set goals or targets.

The results of the analysis were fed back to the key executives in man-power development and personnel. A fairly extensive effort to improve the MBO program was then undertaken to resolve some of these problems.

THE CHANGE PROGRAM

FEEDBACK AND TRAINING FOR TOP-MANAGEMENT GROUP. A meeting was held with the top executive group in the organization. The rationale of MBO was discussed extensively with this group, with the research results cited in Chapter 2 serving as a basis for the discussion. Deficiencies in the existing program were clearly identified by feeding back research results, and some strategies were suggested for change.

THE INTRODUCTION OF A NEW WPR (MBO) FORM. A new form was prepared for use. The old form consisted of a single sheet of paper on which both performance and self-improvement goals were listed. Some space was provided for comments by the superior to indicate the level of goal accomplishment at the end of the year. This single sheet form, in the past, had been carefully typed and was sent to the personnel department at the year's end.

The revised form was of a folder type on quite heavy paper and was intended to serve as a working instrument rather than just as a form to be filed away. It contained sections in which the subordinate's career aspirations and development needs could be treated. In addition, the section for self-improvement goals was separated from the section for performance goals.

THE ARRANGEMENT OF GOAL-SETTING MEETINGS. The most extensive and important part of the change program was the establishment of a series of goal-setting meetings between each superior and all his subordinates. These are the cascading meetings previously described. The first intensive goal-setting meeting was conducted with the chief executive of the firm and the vice-presidents who reported to him. Prior to this meeting, the chief executive had prepared a set of goals that he believed represented the direction that the company should take. He then communicated these goals at the meeting to his subordinates for their information. In addition, at this meeting, the results of the evaluation of the earlier MBO program were presented along with the recommendations for improvement and the new format.

Following this group meeting, each vice-president then developed a set of his own goals. When this had been accomplished, the chief executive met individually with each of the vice-presidents to finalize their goals. Each vice-president in turn communicated his finalized goals to his subordinates at a group meeting, then met individually with them to establish their goals. In a two-week period, approximately forty group meetings were held. These meetings covered managers down to the operating levels in each major organizational division, except one in which the goal-setting process broke down. In this division, relatively little goal setting took place.

At both individual and group meetings at the vice-presidential level, a researcher was present to act in an advisory capacity, explaining the research results and, more importantly, aiding in the goal setting. A representative from the organizational development unit served this function in the other meetings.

THE FOLLOW-UP STUDY. After the new MBO program had been in effect for one year, a follow-up study was conducted with the same instruments and methods as in the initial MBO study. The objective of this follow-up study was to determine if the new MBO program was more effective than the old.

THE SECOND INTERVIEW STUDY

Because of a time lapse of approximately eighteen months between the first and second data collections, two things happened that precluded interviewing the same group of managers included in the first study. First, a number of them changed jobs within the company, which means that they had new bosses whose goal-setting habits could be drastically different from the previous bosses. Second, a number left the company. Nevertheless, approximately forty managers interviewed previously were interviewed again in depth.

The interview schedules were the same, directing the subject toward areas of interest such as the philosophy underlining objectives, problems, how goals were set, and so on. The content of these interviews was analyzed along the same lines as the earlier study and the results compared.

FINDINGS. In the second interview study the main findings were

1. More managers saw MBO as a means of developing the potential of their subordinates than before.
2. Most managers in the first study said that MBO helped them to know what was expected of them. Now most managers said that they were more aware of and gave evidence of knowing more about company goals.

3. The biggest problems with MBO in the first study were excessive formal requirements and the fact that managers were not being utilized to their full potential. In the second study, lack of good feedback was the primary problem with MBO.

DISCUSSION OF FINDINGS. It was quite clear that the organization was doing a better job of communicating its goals to lower levels under the new program than under the old. It also seemed that, as the MBO approach became more ingrained in the organization, managers became so habituated to it that the paper work no longer seemed excessive, even though these requirements were probably higher than before.

One important problem was found in this second series of interviews that was not in the first. Some of the managers reported that they had troubles dealing with the "personal improvement" goals of subordinates. This new problem came about after the introduction of the new forms and the intensive goal-setting effort. Many managers felt particularly obliged to discuss career directions and personal development because these items were not touched on directly in the program. However, there are those who find it difficult to treat these problem areas with subordinates:

How do I deal with someone who has no potential?

What do I do with a senior manager who isn't motivated anymore?

What do you say to the aggressive young fast-tract man who feels he is ready for a job change and may leave if he doesn't get it?

These, and many other problems, are now more obvious to managers using MBO. Many more managers are facing such problems openly, looking for a solution of some sort. As these problems will exist under any circumstances, it is better that they be opened up.

THE SECOND QUESTIONNAIRE STUDY

Approximately 150 managers from all levels and functions received a second questionnaire by mail (see Appendix A). Usable data were obtained from 120 managers in the first administration. In the follow-up administration, usable questionnaires were returned by 110 of the respondents. Approximately 20 per cent of the respondents in the follow-up administration were not included in the first sampling because many managers changed jobs or left between administrations.

It was expected that the newly constructed program would result in certain changes. If the change program were successful, one would expect changes in perceptions of goals and goal setting, the manner and frequency of the review process, and the level of organizational support for the MBO program. Along with these changes, more positive reactions to the MBO program and more success in achieving goals would be expected.

However, one would not expect changes in job characteristics and/or personal characteristics, such as our measure of the need for structure, as these would not be affected by the change program. Neither was it anticipated that perceptions of supervisory style would change, except for increased attention of the superior to the MBO program and perhaps some increase in satisfaction with the boss.

ANALYTICAL METHOD

Mean scores were obtained for each item from the first and second questionnaire administrations. Differences between means were analyzed statistically using t tests. Findings are given in tabular form in Appendix C.

FINDINGS. *Characteristics.* The results indicated that none of the job characteristics changed significantly. Respondents were no more satisfied with pay or their jobs than before. Managers did not report any more control over their work, any changes in their jobs, or more job interest in the after measure than before [see Table C-1 (in Appendix C)].

The Need for Structure. Table C-2 indicates that there was no change in the need for structure, a personality trait, of the respondents.

Goal Characteristics. There appeared to be a fairly substantial change in the manner in which goals were perceived by the respondents (see Table 3). Both performance goals and self-improvement goals were perceived to be more difficult. At the same time the respondents viewed the goals as being important and clear. They also reported that they had a greater number of goals. Subordinates' influence in the establishment of goals did not change.

Feedback Characteristics. Two dimensions of feedback were analyzed—frequency and type (see Table C-4). The nature of the feedback did not change. Managers seemed to be no more or no less critical or praising than before. But there was a change in the perceived frequency of feedback; respondents reported significantly more feedback for both performance goals and self-improvement goals.

Perceptions of the Superior. There was very little change in the perceptions of the subordinates about their bosses (see Table C-5). There was no greater boss involvement in the job of the subordinate; there were no better relationships; the boss was no more helpful in the subordinate's job than before; and there was no increased influence of the subordinate over his job. Superiors were seen as no more capable now than before. The only change, an expected one, was that subordinates perceived their boss as spending more time on MBO than in the past.

Organizational Support for MBO. Subordinates indicated that there was greater support, both from the company and the superior, for MBO than had been the case in the past (see Table C-6). Of course, this result was expected because of the intensive goal-setting effort described earlier.

Changes in Reactions to MBO. Those items that can be described as effect variables in the MBO program also changed, with the exception of perceived goal success. Managers reported that they worked harder at their job than before (see Table C-7), but they also had more positive attitudes toward MBO than in the past. They viewed it as more helpful in their job and as more applicable to their work. This was also predicted.

DISCUSSION OF FINDINGS. After the intensive goal-setting effort, MBO was seen differently by managers. Goals were described as being more clearly stated and more difficult. Managers were more aware of the importance of goals. Changes of this type would lead us to conclude that there is a better understanding and communication of the goals following intensive goal setting. More managers in the organization felt that they knew where the top management "wanted to go" and what their part should be.

Feedback increased in perceived frequency but not in type. Superiors were presumably talking more with subordinates but about the same things. There was no shift in these data in the direction of either more or less criticism or praise in the feedback. This may or may not be a problem. An earlier study suggests that criticism or praise has different effects on an individual, a function perhaps of the personality characteristics.[11]

There were only minor changes in the manner in which the respondents described their work relationships with their superiors. There were no changes in items dealing with general working relationships. Respondents did not feel that their bosses were any more involved with them than in the past. They were no more satisfied with the boss, nor did they feel that their influence was greater than before. This leads us to conclude that perceived managerial style was not altered as a result of intensive goal setting. There is no reason to expect that it should be. Only the perceived amount of time that the boss spent on MBO increased. And this should have because now most subordinates did, in fact, observe superiors working hard at setting goals.

An interesting point that should be noted is the lack of change in what might be called "participation" variables. MBO has been thought of by some as a way to increase participation, or influence, of lower organizational levels. The data suggest that increased influence in goal setting, as described here, did not take place. Perhaps it is more appropriate to view MBO as a method that *can* increase involvement, interaction, and understanding of goals. Increasing participation, in terms of changing degrees of influence of lower-level personnel, requires a more extensive shift in both the philosophy and practice of management and more than an MBO program provides by itself.

There were also some changes in what were designated as end-result variables. Satisfaction with MBO was higher, as was the extent to which managers thought MBO to be helpful in their work. Satisfaction with MBO should be considered an important dimension, as it seems to us that negative attitudes toward it could hinder its general use by managers. The practice of intensive goal setting by top management was associated with positive changes in attitude toward MBO.

There was an increase in "the amount of effort put forth." Managers reported that they worked harder now, more so than before. However, perceived goal success did not change. It may well be that, although goals were more difficult and managers did work harder, they were no more successful at achieving goals than in the past, but the goals were higher, more difficult, and more challenging.

It is interesting to examine our results in light of the earlier follow-up study by Raia,[12] which, one year after the original evaluation, indicated no major shift in the way that the goal setting was handled. We, however, undertook to make a change, and, in our follow-up study, a substantially larger proportion, 53 per cent of those interviewed, felt that they had adequate, or better, information about the relationship of their goals to those of top management. In Raia's research, only one manager felt that it "got lower levels more involved with the company."

Raia also reported a "distortion of managerial philosophy." It seems that some of his managers believed the program to be pressure laden and detrimental to morale. Our data suggest that this did not occur in our study. In our case, the managers seemed more aware of what the philosophy of MBO was, especially with respect to dealing with growth and development goals. Because, as Raia notes, it is important for the program to be made "explicit and become a way of life," and because intensive goal setting was undertaken to integrate MBO into the organization, it seems that a generally satisfactory level of awareness about it developed.

Raia noted too that, even in the second year, the paper-work problem persisted. We found it to be less significant, even though, in fact, there were additional work requirements. This may be because a great deal of time was spent in explaining the process to the managers, and because there was goal setting on a planned basis.

Thus, it would seem that some of the problems and difficulties that Raia reported may have been overcome in our case, with the planned intervention. This was an intensive goal-setting effort, which required a substantial commitment from top management to goal setting. This may be the primary reason for the differences found in the two studies.

SUMMARY

In this chapter we have described the mechanics for implementing MBO and presented research results about MBO in action. Specifically, attention has been directed to those problems of getting managers to understand this approach and to use it. We have not dealt at length with the nature of forms or the specific types of reporting mechanisms to be used in MBO. These should be developed individually to meet the needs of each organization.

Some will argue that our strategy for implementation is an intensively formalized, rigid one. There is no doubt that such is the case. However, it is our experience that unless it is implemented in this manner, MBO is unlikely to be broadly used throughout the organization in its first stages. If formal requirements are not imposed on managers, they will continue to operate in a style and fashion they believe to be appropriate.

Without an implementation process, such as we described above, we do not believe that MBO will be effectively implemented. This is not to say that it cannot work any other way. It is certainly more desirable that MBO become an integrated part of the managerial style and philosophy in the company than not. But we think that this is most likely to happen if there is a fairly well disciplined, formal MBO effort. Perhaps the implementation process that we have described will allow those managers who use it to see its benefits and facilitate their adoption of the process.

The most important key to the implementation of MBO is its use by top management. This is not a system to be used solely by subordinates. To us, there is little question that the participation by top management in MBO is the fundamental factor that governs the effective implementation of such a system, as participation is the best indicator of top-management support. The earlier discussion of our research suggests that satisfaction with MBO is positively related to the manner in which the subordinate feels that MBO is supported, that is, used, by the boss. We believe our research to be strong evidence of the link between managerial support and the degree of acceptance of MBO by an individual. Only when each level of management reinforces the use of MBO for lower levels by using it itself are there any real benefits.

NOTES

1. Wickens, J. D. "Management by Objectives: An Appraisal," *Journal of Management Studies,* **5** (1968), 365–379.
2. Meyer, H. H., E. Kay, and J. R. P. French, Jr. "Split Roles in Performance Appraisal," *Harvard Business Review,* **43** (1965), 123–129.
3. Preston, S. J. "J. Stone's Management by Objectives," *Personnel* (London) **1** (1968), 22–25.
4. Porter, L., and E. Lawler III. *Managerial Attitudes and Performance.* Homewood, Ill.: Irwin, 1968.
5. Ivancevich, J. M., J. H. Donnelly, and L. Lyon. "A Study of the Impact of Management by Objectives on Perceived Need Satisfaction," *Personnel Psychology,* **23** (1970), 139–151.
6. Stein, C. I. Personal communication, Carroll I. Stein and Associates, Minneapolis, Minn., July, 1970.
7. Kepner, C. H., and B. B. Tregoe. *The Rational Manager: A Systematic Approach to Problem Solving and Decision Making.* New York: McGraw Hill, 1965. Maier, N. R., *Problem Solving Discussions and Conferences: Leadership Methods and Skills.* New York: McGraw Hill, 1963.
8. Tosi, H. L., Jr., and S. J. Carroll, Jr. "Managerial Reaction to Management by Objectives," *Academy of Management Journal,* **11** (1968), 415–425.
9. Carroll, S. J., Jr., and H. L. Tosi, Jr. "The Relationship of Characteristics of the Review Process as Moderated by Personality and Situational Factors to the Success of the 'Management by Objectives' Approach," *Proceedings, Academy of Managmeent,* 1969.
10. Tosi and Carroll, 1968, op. cit.
11. Carroll and Tosi, 1969, op. cit.
12. Raia, A. P. "A Second Look at Goals and Controls," *California Management Review,* **8** (1966), 49–58.

4

*SETTING GOALS IN MBO**

MBO is a process in which members of complex organizations, working in conjunction with one another, identify common goals and coordinate their efforts toward achieving them. Emphasis is on the future and change, since an objective or goal (used synonymously herein) is a state or a condition to be achieved at some future time. Emphasis is on where the organization is going—the what and the how of its intended accomplishments. Objectives can be thought of as statements of purpose and direction, formalized into a system of management. They may be long-range or short-range. They may be general, to provide direction to an entire organization, or they may be highly specific, to provide detailed direction for a given individual.

One purpose of MBO is to facilitate the derivation of specific

* This chapter is based on an article by the authors and John Rizzo entitled "Setting Goals in Management by Objectives." © 1970 by The Regents of the University of California. Reprinted from *California Management Review*, Vol. 12, No. 4, pp. 70–78, by permission of The Regents.

objectives from general ones so that objectives at all levels in the organization are both appropriate to each level and also linked to each other. A set of objectives for an organizational unit is the basis that determines its activities. A set of objectives for an individual determines his job and can be thought of as a different way to provide a job description. Once objectives are determined and assumed by organizational units and by individuals, it is possible to work out the means, or performance, required for accomplishing the objectives. Following this process, methods of achieving objectives, resources required, timing, interactions with others, control, and evaluation must be attended to on a continuing basis.

Objectives may or may not require change. The goal may be one of ensuring that no change occurs in, for example, an important recurring organizational operation. But the emphasis still remains on change and the future, and "no-change" conditions can be thought of as making finer change discriminations in the management process. Even so, MBO is deemed most appropriate in situations where activities tend not to be recurring or repetitive, where change toward new or improved conditions is sought. Typically, these would be innovative endeavors, problem-solving situations, improvements, and personal development.

Objectives may originate at any point in the organizational structure. Quite naturally, they should be derived from the general purposes of the organizations and be consistent with its philosophy, policies, and plans. MBO should obviously be an integral part of the policy formulation and planning process. For example, a given over-all plan can specify the phasing and timing of organizational operations, out of which are derived objectives for particular units. Objectives are not considered as substitutes for plans but rather as a basis for developing them. The stating of objectives accomplishes the following:

1. It documents expectations in the superior–subordinate relationship regarding what is to be done and the level of attainment for the period covered by the goal.
2. It provides members with a firmer base for developing and integrating plans and personal and departmental activity.
3. It serves as the basis for feedback and evaluation of the subordinate's performance.
4. It provides for coordination and timing of individual and unit activities.
5. It draws attention to the need for the control of key organizational functions.
6. It provides a basis for work-related rewards as opposed to personality-based systems.

7. It emphasizes change, improvement, and growth of the organization and the individual.

AN APPROACH FOR ESTABLISHING GOALS AT THE TOP LEVEL OF THE ORGANIZATION[1]

Goals for the organization as a whole are obviously the most difficult of all organizational goals to establish. Such goals must of necessity be based on premises about the future and on a clear understanding of the organization's strengths and weaknesses and those of any present or future competitors. One approach for establishing such organizational goals for an industrial firm might be as follows:

1. Evaluate the future economic outlook for the organization. This process will include an analysis of product strengths and weaknesses in various markets.
2. Evaluate the organization itself. This process will include an analysis of organizational structure, strengths and weaknesses in human resources, and the financial constraints to which the organization is subject.
3. List the major opportunities and problems facing the organization in the near and far future.
4. Devise programs for taking advantage of the opportunities and for solving the organization's problems.
5. Convert these programs to resource needs and to financial statements for the current year and the next several years.
6. Revise programs as necessary and establish objectives for the organization.

These organizational objectives are then communicated downward, as indicated previously. Stages in the programs necessary to accomplish organizational objectives become objectives for individuals and for their organizational units.

OBJECTIVES AS MEANS–END DISTINCTIONS

The formulation of objectives through an organization represents a kind of means–end analysis, which is an attempt to factor general requirements into specific activities. Means–end analysis includes establishing

the general goal to be achieved, . . . discovering a set of means, very generally specified, for accomplishing this goal, . . . taking each of these means, in turn, as a new sub-goal and discovering a more detailed set of means for achieving it, etc.[2]

MBO is predicated on this concept. It is assumed that a means–end analysis can occur with a degree of precision and accuracy. The end represents a condition or situation that is desired, a purpose to be achieved, and can be equated with goal or objective. Objectives may represent required inputs to other sectors of the organization. They may be specific achievement levels, such as production costs, sales volume, and so on. They may also be completed projects. For instance, the market research department may seek to complete a sales forecast by a particular date so that the production facilities may be properly coordinated with market demands. Objectives, or end states, are attained through the performance of some activity; activities are the means to achieve the end. It is important to distinguish between ends and means in the use of the objectives approach, as there are implications for measurement and assessment that will be discussed later.

It is obvious that a malfunction or break in such a process may lead to major problems in the implementation of MBO. It is for this reason that commitment, effort, support, and use by top management is critical at all levels to obtain consensus of objectives, cooperation in achievement, and the use of objectives as criteria for evaluation.

STATEMENT OF THE OBJECTIVE

The objectives for any position should reflect the means–end distinction discussed earlier. The first critical phase in setting objectives is the statement that describes the end state sought. This statement should be

1. Clear, concise, and unambiguous.
2. Accurate in terms of the true end state or condition sought.
3. Consistent with policies, procedures, and plans as they apply to the unit.
4. Within the competence of the man, or represent a reasonable learning and developmental experience for him.
5. Interesting, motivating, and/or challenging whenever possible.

Some examples of goal statements that might be written are

1. Increase sales by 10 per cent.
2. Reduce manufacturing costs by 5 per cent.

3. Reduce customer complaints.
4. Increase sales by 5 per cent by December 1.
5. Increase quality within a 5 per cent increase in production control costs.
6. Develop understanding and implementation of computer techniques among subordinates.

Notice that these statements have at least two key components. First, each on the list clearly suggests an area of activity in which accomplishment takes place. Second, some clearly specify a level of achievement, the quantity or deadlines to be met. We shall refer to the desired level of achievement as the performance level. The need for this distinction is obvious; it indicates the evaluation criterion by specifying the level and/or the condition that should exist. This has clear implications for both measurement and appraisal. Before discussing these implications, however, we need a more detailed examination of the scope and types of objectives in the MBO process.

THE SCOPE AND TYPE OF OBJECTIVES

It would be difficult to conceive of developing objectives for a manager that would cover each and every area of responsibility, as the task structure of most jobs is simply too complex. Yet, once objectives are set for a position, they should comprise the major description of the job, and the probability of their achievement should be assessed in light of what is known about total job requirements. Any feeling of conflict between objectives and other job requirements should be prevented.

Two major types of objectives may be delineated: performance objectives and personal development objectives.* Performance objectives refer mainly to those goals and activities that relate to the individual's position assignment. Personal development goals have to do with increasing the individual's skills, job knowledge, or potential. More importantly, the delineation of types of objectives in this manner allows for an assessment of how MBO is being used and what aspects of it are being emphasized; for instance,

1. Once all objectives are set for a person, a basis exists to ensure that there is a "balance" of different types, that he is solving problems, developing, and maintaining critical functions.

---

* These categories are similar to those proposed by G. Odiorne. See his *Management by Objectives*. New York: Pitman, 1964; especially Chapters 7, 8, and 9.

2. Some estimates can be made regarding the importance of objectives and the consequences of failure to achieve them. For example, a man who fails on a difficult performance objective should not be evaluated in the same way as one who fails to maintain a critical recurring operation.

PERFORMANCE OBJECTIVES. Performance objectives derive directly from the job assignment, that is, from the major areas of responsibility and activity of the individual. Among them would be the maintenance of recurring or routine activities, the solving of problems, or the creation of innovative ideas, products, services, and the like.

Some of these objectives may take the form of special activities or projects not normally part of the job—for example, emergencies, changes in priorities, or simply management decisions. It is of course also true that what is a special activity for one position may be routine for another. A special-project goal for a lower-level manager might be a routine goal for his boss. The development of the computer-based information system for personnel records may be highly creative objectives for the personnel department, yet could be considered a routine goal for a systems analysis group.

Discretionary Areas and Other Problems. By its very nature, organization imposes restrictions on individuals. The structure of an organization defines legitimate areas of influence and decision making for a manager. Specialization and definition of function tends to limit decisions and activities to those defined for the incumbent.

A lower-level manager cannot legitimately influence goal levels and action plans in areas in which he has no discretion, unless he has the approval of his superior. Therefore, it is necessary to spell out areas in which the subordinate has discretion so that he knows what his decision limits are. Otherwise, the manager may be misled into believing that he can participate in departmental and organizational decisions that have been defined, either procedurally or by managerial fiat, as being outside his discretion area. When one develops expectancies that participation is legitimate and these are not reinforced, negative consequences may occur.

One way to define discretion areas is to determine whether an individual should influence means or ends. If the activity operates primarily across the boundaries of the organization and is affected by conditions beyond its control, the individual charged with performing it may be in a better position to determine both the goals (or ends) and the most appropriate manner of achieving them. For instance, the marketing executive in constant touch with the external environment is in a better position to determine possible sales penetration and programs than others in the organization. Therefore, not having discretion over goal levels should not preclude his involvement in goal setting. The MBO process will focus, however, on the development of the best means (or action plans) for goal attainment.

High levels of skill and technology required in a particular function may make the specialist better able to assess what can be done in a technical field than a nontechnical person. Thus, he should be involved in the determination of goal levels, as well as in the carrying out of activities. In general, however, organizational constraints and requirements, such as budget limitations, sales quotas, and production requirements, are boundaries or restrictions that may not be removed, although they may have to be more flexible under the conditions discussed above.

On the other hand, if performance levels are set, for any reason, at higher organization levels, there is little option but to focus on the determination of the "best" activities to achieve these levels. Internal definition of goal levels will most probably be for activities that function primarily within the boundaries of the organization. The assumption, of course, is that the person defining the objective, or level, is either competent to do so or must because of its critical importance.

An important limitation on discretion is organizational level. As one moves to lower levels of the organization, the manager's zone of discretion becomes more and more narrow. That is, the manager at the lower levels is responsible generally for a fewer number of activities and can commit smaller quantities of resources than those at higher levels. Thus, activities at lower levels tend to be more specific, and tend to be measurable.[3]

Another factor that causes variation in the discretion range is the changing competence of the incumbent. When one is learning a job, he may need more guidance from the superior. However, as his skills increase, the superior may spend less time with him, as the subordinate can capably handle more activities and make more decisions. The objectives approach, incidentally, may help the superior make assessments of the subordinate's competence. As the subordinate becomes more successful in achieving goals, additional and more challenging goals, within the parameters of the job, can be added. When the incumbent can perform these adequately, consideration should be given to possible promotion and transfer.

What about those areas beyond the discretion limits? We are not suggesting that the subordinate should have no part in these decisions. This role may be the contribution of information and assistance, providing inputs to the decision-making process of the superior. But this type of activity must be differentiated from goal-setting participation, in which the individual has something to say about the final shape and form of the goals and activities.

However, discretion boundaries are not rigid. Although a particular decision may fall within a subordinate's discretion range under normal circumstances, emergencies may develop that result in the decision's being made by the boss. These conditions cannot be foreseen and consequently are not planned for.

We have indicated elsewhere the relationships between personality characteristics and goals. Difficult goals, for example, were found to result in positive motivation for subordinates high in self-esteem. The development of a positive self-concept for individuals, then, is important. In the interim, special care should be taken to increase goal clarity for managers with lower levels of job interest and to give specific information on the relative priority of goals to managers high in need for structure.

PERSONAL DEVELOPMENT OBJECTIVES. First, it is important to stress that personal development objectives must be based on problems or deficiencies, current or anticipated, in such areas as technical skills, interpersonal relations, or job changes. The critical nature of these objectives lies in their potential as means to combat obsolescence under a rapid expansion of knowledge, to prepare people for increased responsibility, and to overcome problems in organizational interactions.

Setting development goals is probably more difficult than setting performance goals because the former are personal in nature and, as such, must be handled with care and tact. This difficulty can be avoided by simply not setting them. It could be argued that they should be avoided, as they are an intrusion into the individual's privacy by the boss or the organization. However, when perceived personal limitations hinder effective performance, the problem must be treated in some manner.

Thus, if at any time the superior believes that an individual's limitations stand clearly in the way of the unit's goal achievement, it should be made known to the individual. He may not be aware that he is creating problems and would gladly change—if he knew. Many technically competent people have been relieved from positions because of human problems that they ostensibly create; many of them might have been retained had they only known that problems existed or were developing.

Personal development goals are important to use for correcting performance deficiencies. Research has demonstrated that negative feedback or knowledge of results is not likely in itself to lead to improved performance. The study conducted by Meyer, Kay, and French at General Electric indicated that criticism of subordinates' performances was not sufficient in itself to bring about improvement.[4] Only when performance deficiencies were converted to specific performance-improvement objectives were positive improvements achieved. The series of studies conducted by Locke and Bryan cited in Chapter 1 indicated also that improvements in performance occurred only as a result of goal setting by the individual and not as a result of merely providing the individual with information on his present and past performance. In retrospect, this all seems perfectly logical. Why should knowledge of results alone result in improved performance? Before performance improvement can take place, the individual must have an intention to improve and must have a specific target or standard to use in evaluating his efforts. Objectives serve to mobilize and direct the energy of the individual.

Personal development goals should be based on actual performance deficiencies. If they are included only to meet formal program requirements and are not problem based, they will be of little value. In such a case, personal improvement goals will probably be general and ambiguous, and tenable only if the organization wishes to invest in "education for education's sake." Therefore, unless they are philosophically or value based, personal development goals should attack deficiencies related to performance, containing specific action proposals for solving the problems.

Pinpointing a Problem Area. Parties involved in goal setting should continually be alert to any difficulties resulting from an employee's personal or technical incapacities. The boss is in a particularly important position for recognizing problems, and should therefore attempt to determine the cause of these problems. In addition, those with whom an individual interacts may be in a reasonably good position to judge his technical competence or to determine when problems are due to his behavior. If colleagues are continually complaining about another, additional investigation into the problem is warranted. Another important source of knowledge as to any difficulties is the subordinate himself. He may be very aware of problems in which he is involved and by discussing them may determine those in which he has been the primary cause. An additional source of information for personal development goals is the final review session when reasons for lack of goal accomplishment are being discussed.

Negative incidents should be relatively significant in effect and frequency and not simply a single case that has caused some notice to be taken. This does not mean, however, that an important incident occurring once should be overlooked if it suggests serious deficiencies.

There are at least three areas in which personal development objectives should be set:

1. *Improvement of interpersonal skills.* An inability to maintain reasonably effective work relationships may be due to an individual's lack of awareness or his inability to cooperate. These may rise from personality deficiencies or simple lack of awareness of his impact upon others. He may be unable to recognize that he is precipitating problems.
2. *Improvement of technical skills.* A manager may be, for instance, unable to prepare a budget or engage in research because

he has not had adequate training in these technical areas, or because of new technical developments that could lead to obsolescence. This limitation may not preclude generally acceptable performance, but if skills are improved or increased, results may also be improved.

3. *Preparation for advancement.* Another possibility covers either technical or human skills required for different or higher-level positions. These are truly developmental goals, which focus on preparation for advancement. There are many ways in which they may be achieved. In some cases, the individual may be given advanced work assignments; in others, these goals may be achieved by exposure in training situations to new concepts. In any event, they represent a potential problem area.

Assessing the Causes of the Problem. Once it has been established that a problem exists, the causes need to be determined. Causes should be sought in an investigation and discussion by both the superior and the subordinate after both have given some prior thought to the possible causes. The possible causes of problems may be grouped into three general categories:

1. *Procedures and structure.* The structure of the organization itself may induce disturbances. Interpersonal conflict may develop because of the interdependence of work activities. For instance, if formal requirements are such that they cause a delay in transmission of information, those who need it may develop negative attitudes and feelings, which consequently result in hostility and misunderstanding toward other individuals or units.

2. *Other parties with whom an individual must work.* Problems with subordinates at lower organizational levels or managerial peers of the goal setter may be due to personality incompatibility or the others' lack of certain technical skills. Although this may represent an important cause of problems, it is too easy to blame negative incidents on others.

3. *The person himself.* The individual may have habits and characteristics that are not compatible with those of his subordinates or colleagues. Or, he may lack the technical skills requisite to carry out certain responsibilities.

The attempt to define problems and causes facilitates the conversion of development objectives into achievable goals. Like other objectives, they can be general (attend a sensitivity training course or role-playing seminar) or more specific (attend *XYZ* course in financial planning, use PERT techniques on Project *X*).

A Final Point on Personal Development Objectives. Self-improvement goals may be designed to improve current performance or may be specifically intended to develop skills required at higher levels or in different jobs. In the latter case, it may be impossible to describe the end state of affairs to be achieved upon the completion of the activity, because success can be determined only in the future, or in other positions.

For development objectives, it is necessary to simply rely upon the determination that the action plan has been carried out and that the individual has learned something. Suppose, for instance, that development goals for an engineer, destined to be an engineer supervisor, read as follows:

> To meet with members of the financial, marketing, and production groups in order to learn how product release schedules affect their areas.

Currently, he may have to know little about this, as he may now have little impact on product release schedules. The question then arises: How do you know that the activity produced the desired learning? You don't. It is a simple matter to determine whether or not the meeting was held. It is yet another matter to assess whether or not any learning has occurred. This can only be done by the superior in his role as coach and teacher. At some point in time, the superior, who presumably has some knowledge in the goal area, should discuss the results of the meeting with the subordinate, emphasizing particularly the important points that should have been learned. In this manner, the subordinate will have had the learning experience of the meeting and reinforcement from the discussion with his superior.

There is obviously no way to determine if these activities will either improve the current or future performance of the manager. Managerial judgment is important here. We must simply assume that the superior is able to work with the subordinate to define activities of value in future work assignments.

Finally, it should be clear from the foregoing that performance and development objectives may well be derived from and related to management training and development efforts. These efforts must be designed in a manner that (1) accounts for current organizational problems and future needs, and (2) treats development as an integrated organization-wide effort. MBO should therefore be integrally tied to these objectives.

PERFORMANCE REQUIRED: THE ACTION PLAN

One way to overcome some of the problems inherent in MBO is to have some statement and discussion of the specifics required to accomplish an objective. Earlier, we differentiated means and ends: goal statements reflected the ends. Here, the performance or "action plan" refers to the means for the accomplishment of an objective. These means reflect alternatives, selected perhaps from several, that lead to the desired performance level.

It is in this area that decision making becomes important. For instance, two alternative methods might be suggested to effectively increase market shares. One plan might call for redesigning current products. Another might be to design, develop, and market new products. The various types of costs of the two alternatives—time, material, financial, and human resources, along with other indirect costs—must be evaluated. Cost–benefit analysis must be applied to each alternative, at least in an informal way, in order to maximize the present value of the benefits, less the costs. The alternative with the greater return generally should be selected.

THE ACTION PLAN

Statements of the action plan may be brief but should summarize what will be done. If the activity is complex, the action plan should be broken down into major subprograms, or components. The action plan represents the "best" alternative, possibly of many, that could achieve the goal level. It should represent at least a first approximation of what will be done to achieve the objective. Obviously it is not intended to restrict action to such an extent that it precludes shifting to another strategy if there is a need to do so. The action plan will provide an initial basis for developing a total action program for the individual or department. Possible action plans are as follows:

> *For an increase in sales:*
> Develop more penetration in a particular market area by increasing the number of calls to dealers there.
> *For reduced manufacturing costs:*
> Analyze the overtime activities and costs, and schedule more work during regular hours.

When a manager has developed action plans or means to achieve his objectives, subordinates may use them as bases for formulating their own and as guides for determining their roles in the unit's effort. Thus, clear differentiation of means from ends can facilitate lower-level use of the objectives process.

Including both means and ends permits not only a comparison of performance against definite criteria but also a determination of whether events leading to the realization of goals took place. This distinction has important implications for the problem of measurement and appraisal (discussed in greater detail in the next section). The effective coordination of one's own activities with the requirements of other sectors of the organization is sometimes neither measurable nor adequately verifiable. Yet, implicitly and intuitively, we know what must be done. Then, if we have distinguished between means and ends, we can determine or verify if the means, or activities, have occurred. It is important to recognize the distinction between measuring an objective and determining whether or not an event has occurred. If we are unable to quantify or specify the goal level adequately, we simply assume that the desired goal level will be achieved if a particular event or set of activities takes place. For example, although it is very difficult to measure, by means of any hard criteria, whether a manager is developing the talents of subordinates, we can determine if he has provided them with development opportunities. If they have participated in seminars, attended meetings, or gone off to school, it may be assumed that the development activity is being properly conducted.

Adequate attention to an action plan provides the following additional benefits and opportunities:

1. It aids in the search for better, more efficient methods of accomplishing the objective.
2. It provides an opportunity to test the feasibility of accomplishing the objective as stated.
3. It develops a sounder basis to estimate time and/or cost required and deadline for accomplishment.
4. It creates an opportunity to examine the nature and degree to which one will have to rely on other people in the organization for coordination and support (see below).
5. It uncovers anticipated snags or barriers to accomplishment.
6. It determines the resources (man power, equipment, supplies, facilities) required to accomplish the objectives.
7. It facilitates control if the performance is well specified and agreed upon; reporting need only occur when problems arise in implementing. This is a form of planning ahead; when plans are sufficiently complete, only deviations from it need be communicated.

8. It identifies areas in which the superior can provide support and assistance.
9. It facilitates the delegation process.

THE DETERMINATION OF COORDINATING REQUIREMENTS AND CONTINGENCIES. In some cases, successful achievement of an objective depends upon the contribution and performance of other individuals or departments. If these are not forthcoming at the proper time, or in the proper amount, the project may fail. Thus, since they may be extremely critical to successful performance, they must be taken into account.

Some contingencies apply to all objectives and need not be discussed with regard to each objective. For example, delays in the availability of resources, changes in support or priorities from higher management, equipment failures, delayed approval, and the like, which are not planned for, are not relevant to one's responsibility for the accomplishment of objectives.

Other contingencies, specific to the objective, should be discussed. Among these might be inadequate authority of the subordinate, lack of policy covering certain aspects of the objective, possible failure to gain other's cooperation, known relevant delays in the system, and so on. Once these are uncovered, several actions are possible:

1. Re-examination of the objective (for example, alteration of a deadline) when and if the contingency occurs.
2. Commitment of the superior to help by overcoming or preventing the contingency.
3. Revision of the performance required to accomplish the objective.
4. The establishment of a new objective. If a contingency is serious enough, an objective aimed at overcoming the problem may be justified.

PROBLEMS OF MEASUREMENT AND APPRAISAL

MBO carries with it most of the familiar difficulties and complications of measurement and appraisal processes. Its emphasis on performance, as opposed to personality traits or criteria presumed to be related to performance, makes it potentially more effective. But this potential cannot be realized unless, as is true with any approach, measurement and appraisal are reasonably valid, reliable, objective, and equitable.

MEANS, ENDS, AND EVALUATION

Evaluations should rarely be based simply on whether or not the objective is accomplished, or on the sheer number of objectives accomplished (although both may be considered). Appraisal of performance should take into account

1. Quantitative aspects. (Was cost reduced 5 per cent as planned?)
2. Qualitative aspects. (Have good relations been established with department X? Has an evaluation technique been established?)
3. Deadline considerations. (Was the deadline beaten? Was it met?)
4. Proper allocation of time to formation of objectives.
5. Type and difficulty of objectives.
6. Creativity in overcoming obstacles.
7. Additional objectives suggested or undertaken.
8. Efficient use of resources.
9. Use of good management practices in accomplishing objectives (cost reduction, delegation, good planning, and so on).
10. Coordinative and cooperative behavior; avoidance of conflict-inducing or unethical practices.

It is evident that evaluation and measurement require consideration of the means of achieving, as well as the ends sought. Thus, concern must be given to both the objective (number, type, difficulty, and so on) and the manner in which it is achieved (cost, cooperation, time consumed, and the like). Unless this is done, an important opportunity to communicate expectations, to give precise feedback on performance results, and to set effective goals may be lost. It must be fully understood that evaluation has obvious links to action plans as well as to desired end states.

ADDITIONAL CONSIDERATIONS OF MEASUREMENT

There are some goals that lend themselves more easily to measurement than others, such as scrap rates, production costs, sales volume, and other "hard" measures. Unfortunately, these are neither relevant nor applicable to all jobs, or even to the majority of activities that make up most jobs. These measurements seem to be most appropriate to lower levels of the organization and in areas such as production, marketing, or other major functional activities of the organization. They are less applicable in most staff and specialist units. The measurement problem often reduces to finding the appropriate, agreed-upon criteria for each objective, realizing that some will apply to many situations, whereas others are unique to a single objective.

We have already detailed the distinction between performance and personal development objectives. Another distinction, relevant to the measurement problem, is discussed here: the difference between routine and special project objectives. Classifying objectives according to these types permits some important refinements in evaluation and control. By examining the nature of the mix of objectives for a set of positions, it is possible to determine any or all of the following:

1. The extent to which each individual has some personal development objectives.
2. If sufficient problem solving or innovative activities were forthcoming in units where they might be required.
3. The determination of priorities for performance and/or personal development objectives.

Routine objectives are those derived from the basic responsibilities of the job. They have to do with those activities that comprise the core of the job description. How they should be measured is an important question. The most appropriate method for evaluating whether or not an individual has achieved them is to first ensure that he is aware of these activities and required levels. The manager must communicate to the subordinate, at some point early in their relationship, the major activities of the job and what the desired level of performance is. These should be made known to the individual prior to any assessment of the individual's performance, so that an individual is not evaluated ex post facto. Often an individual is not aware of the criteria that the manager used in the evaluation until evaluation actually occurs.

At the same time that the criteria are being specified, the boss should develop tolerance limits that are acceptable to him, for, although measurement of the routine should be a major part of the objectives process, it should be of most concern when performance falls outside acceptable levels. Essentially, we are proposing that minimum performance levels be set for routine activities, and only performance that falls below these minimums be noted. Therefore, evaluation of routine goals is by exception, or when these standards are not met. Naturally, the ability to manage by exception is, to a great extent, contingent upon the existence of good plans or clear standards from which exceptions can be specified in advance. Odiorne cites the following example:

> The paymaster, for example, may report that his routine duties cluster around getting the weekly payroll out every Friday. It is agreed that

the measure of exception will be zero—in other words, the boss should expect no exceptions to the diligent performance of this routine duty. Thus, the failure any week to produce the payroll on Friday will be considered an exception that calls for explanation by the subordinate. If the cause were reasonably under his control or could have been averted by extra care or effort, the absence of the payroll will be considered a failure on the part of the subordinate.[5]

What about performance that exceeds the desired levels? When a subordinate frequently exceeds the performance levels, the manager should make him aware that his outstanding performance has been observed. Positive feedback should occur, especially to let the individual know when he is performing his major job responsibilities exceptionally well.

Generally, routine job responsibilities or goals will be expressed as job standards, or other "hard" performance measures. Essentially, appraisal and evaluation will be based on the comparison of performance to the standard. This type of evaluation alone, however, may be relatively short-sighted and suboptimal. Recall that the manager should also evaluate the manner in which performance was carried out. For example, the reduction of costs by foregoing other expenditures may have negative long-run effects. In the same way, there can be substantial distortions of accomplishment when only quantitative criteria are used in measurement.

Problem-solving, special-project, or *creative objectives* present another type of problem. Obviously, for these activities it is more difficult to develop quantified measures of performance than for the essentially routine. If the ends are truly creative, the determination of whether an adequate performance level is attained may be necessarily based on an intuitive judgment, in that innovation and invention are needed in the very formulation of such objectives. Hence, we cannot generally measure results in these areas adequately and/or directly. It is usually possible, however, to judge if an activity has been performed in some appropriate manner, even though the ends, or the performance levels, are neither quantifiable nor measurable. For example, we can assess whether or not an activity has occurred by some specific point in time or whether or not a specific dollar amount has been expended. Thus, we are not only concerned with whether or not events have occurred but also within some tolerance limit, such as that of target dates, budget constraints, or a quality assessment by the manager. It does become possible under these conditions to establish review points and therefore to give attention to the outcome of activities when they occur. Deliberations on these outcomes can then serve as a re-evaluation of both the objectives and the means, thus making changes possible. Finally, both flexibility and control are assured where they appear to be most needed—when predictions, plans, and standards could not be specified or articulated in advance.

A NOTE ON DEADLINES AND BUDGET

Deadlines and/or budget constraints can be strictly specified in some cases and not in others. A great deal will depend on

1. The importance of the objective.
2. The ability to predict the actual time or costs that will be required in performance.
3. Whether or not written plans or objectives of other people require coordinated completion dates.
4. The amount of time and money required by the particular objective under discussion.
5. The predictability of problems or barriers to accomplishment.

Discussion of these constraints allows greater understanding between superiors and subordinates and establishes how they will be used in evaluation. Expectations become known; realities can be tested. Deadlines and costs should be viewed as negotiable, and should be reasonably and rationally arrived at whenever possible. Deadlines especially should not be set simply to ensure that performance be initiated toward an objective.

We wish to re-emphasize the fundamental importance in MBO of the development and utilization of sound criteria for evaluation, appraisal, and feedback. This is critical to the achievement of meaningful changes in behavior. Yet heavy reliance upon hard criteria—measurable or identifiable factors or changes, such as production levels, market share, sales volume, turnover, and grievance rates—requires extreme care. After all, grievance rates can be reduced simply by capitulating and not allowing complaints to advance to or beyond the first grievance stage. Production costs may be kept at a minimum by delaying necessary preventive maintenance programs. We can see therefore that hard criteria are best viewed as ends or levels because they indicate nothing about the *means* of attaining goals. Soft criteria, on the other hand, do not involve a particular level of achievement but rather determine whether or not an event or condition has come about. They may involve intuitive evaluation of the ability of a subordinate to achieve the desired performance level, or whether or not the subordinate's plan for action will achieve the desired quality on a particular project. Soft criteria are a vital and fundamental part of MBO. Without them, the approach cannot be well implemented.

To some managers, the development and communication of goals comes naturally. There are those who are able to intuitively determine and specify appropriate measures, criteria, and goals, along with the most satisfactory methods for achieving them. These managers sense what must be observed and measured, and communicate this effectively to subordinates. This, of course, is the behavior that MBO seeks to develop and reinforce.

SUMMARY

The chapter details the problem of setting goals for individual managers and organizational units, points out that action plans should be developed for each objective, and lists the advantages of using both objectives and action plans in management. It presents the different types of constraints limiting a manager's discretion and discusses the importance of communicating these to the managers involved. It also treats in general terms both the difficulties in measuring performance of assigned objectives and methods of overcoming these problems. The next chapter presents a more complete description of approaches for reviewing performance under an MBO program.

NOTES

1. Humble, J. W. *Management by Objectives.* London: Industrial Education and Research Foundation, 1967.
2. March, J., and H. Simon. *Organizations.* New York: Wiley, 1959, p. 191.
3. Tosi, H. L., Jr. and S. J. Carroll, Jr., "Some Structural Factors Related to Goal Influence in the Management by Objectives Process," *Business Topics,* Spring 1969, pp. 45–50.
4. Meyer, H. H., E. Kay, and J. R. P. French. "Split Roles in Performance Appraisal," *Harvard Business Review,* **43** (1965), 123–129.
5. Odiorne, G. *Management by Objectives.* New York: Pitman, 1964, p. 104.

5

CARRYING OUT THE REVIEW PROCESS UNDER MBO

In MBO two different kinds of review sessions should be used: intermediate reviews of progress to date and the final review of goal accomplishment.

OBJECTIVES OF THE INTERMEDIATE REVIEW

The primary purpose of the intermediate review is to determine whether the subordinate is progressing satisfactorily toward the completion of performance and personal development goals. If not, some corrective action must be taken. If the subordinate's interest is flagging, or if he has run into a bottleneck or barrier beyond his control, pressure or support from the boss or additional resources may alleviate the problem. Or it may be necessary to change the goals or targets themselves, if conditions now exist that make them unreasonable. However, as indicated earlier, if goals are adjusted too frequently, the effectiveness and usefulness of the objectives approach may be reduced.

The intermediate review may provide other benefits. For example, by determining why goals are not being achieved at a satisfactory level or rate of progress, problems in the organization may be identified that otherwise might remain hidden.

In addition, the increased opportunity for superior–subordinate interaction will help both individuals to get to know each other better. Greater mutual esteem may result, which in turn, may improve the future motivational influence of the superior when exceptional progress toward goals is rewarded through prompt recognition.

This review session may also increase the clarity of assigned performance and development goals. It is too easy for both the superior and subordinate to leave the original goal-setting session believing that a mutual understanding of the goals has been established, when such is actually not the case. This may be especially true in the case of personal development goals.

Finally, the intermediate review adds flexibility to the MBO process. Organizational and environmental factors sometimes change, causing what was once the best means or action plan for a particular result to be now the second, third or fifth best way to accomplish an objective. The superior and his subordinate can thus use these review sessions to work out new approaches to the realization of goals.

OBJECTIVES OF THE FINAL REVIEW

At the final review session, an assessment is made of which goals were successfully accomplished and how well they were achieved, considering the importance and difficulty of each goal for the manager. During this review, it is especially important to minimize defensiveness on the part of the subordinate.

BEHAVIORAL PROBLEMS IN CONDUCTING THE PERFORMANCE REVIEW

The review process is more likely to be carried out effectively and to achieve its objectives when both participants understand something about why people behave as they do in an evaluation interview. Although clear communication is helpful, each party will evaluate the information content of any discussion in terms of his own needs and perceptions.

COMMUNICATION PROBLEMS

In a sense, many problems develop because of communication failures between boss and subordinate. Semantic problems may arise when one party imputes different meanings to words than the other. Either party may lack verbal fluency and thus be unable to adequately express in words what is on his mind. Communication problems may develop because the superior may not have established clearly what information he wants. Either the superior or subordinate may be so concerned about what he wants to say that he does not pay enough attention to what the other is saying. Dislike of the superior may cause the subordinate to misinterpret what is being said. The superior may overestimate the capacity of the other to absorb information.

A situation that can prove troublesome is when feelings about a subject are mixed up with facts about the subject. Statements based on feelings, if interpreted as facts, may seriously distort reality. For example, an individual may be expressing wishful thinking rather than facts when he says: "He'll do anything for me," or "Yes, I know that approach quite well." If the superior takes these statements as true and subsequently acts upon them, serious confusion may result. Sometimes, behavioral gestures are interpreted by the other party in an unintended way. For example, silence, depending on a number of conditions, may be interpreted as understanding when no understanding was intended. A look at the clock may be interpreted as boredom, impatience, or a hint to leave. A raised eyebrow may be interpreted as a sign of disapproval.

PERCEPTIONS

Individuals function on the basis of their perceptions of reality rather than on the basis of "objective" reality. Furthermore, perceptions of reality may be distorted by needs and defense mechanisms. One may see the causes of his failure in the actions of others rather than in his own performance. Perceptions are also affected by what others tell us. One subordinate might tell another that their boss is unreceptive to communications, thus adding to difficulties in communication. A superior who is very insecure might review performance too frequently and demand excessive information from sub-ordinates on goal progress. In addition, he might allow his subordinates only limited latitude in carrying out their assignments. The subordinate may well interpret the boss's behavior as lack of trust. On the other hand, insecure subordinates might react to very casual comments of the superior with great fear and anxiety, leading him to repress information that might reflect adversely on him.

DEFENSIVE REACTIONS

Individuals have certain needs and tend to behave in a manner appropriate for satisfying these needs. Some of these more general needs are for

1. *Security.* The individual needs to feel safe and secure. He prefers to live in a predictable environment that is free from threat and uncertainty. He dislikes being subject to arbitrary or capricious forces that are beyond his control.
2. *Social acceptance.* The individual feels a need to be accepted by others, to belong, to be understood by others, for others to be concerned about him.
3. *Esteem.* The individual needs to feel that he is a worthwhile person. In addition, the individual wants to be respected and looked up to by others.

Some of these needs may be threatened in the evaluation interview, which may lead to defensive reactions by the subordinate. Frustration is the inability to satisfy needs that the individual feels are important. It may stimulate the individual to think up alternative methods of need satisfaction, or he may resort to defense mechanisms, which are methods for coping with unsatisfied needs. Defensive behavior is quite natural and helps the individual adapt to the world. But defense mechanisms often seriously distort reality in such a way that self-esteem or esteem of others is maintained. "Repression" is a form of behavior in which a subordinate may completely forget to report a mistake or an error that he has made. "Rationalization" occurs when an acceptable or "rational" reason for failure is used, even though it is not the cause. For example, a subordinate may give many "acceptable" reasons for avoiding a particularly difficult assignment, when the real reason is fear of failure. Any one of these reactions can occur in the interview.

SOME GENERAL GUIDES FOR REVIEWING PERFORMANCE

Although it is difficult to provide a precise "recipe" for the performance review, some guides can be drawn from the research conducted on appraisal methods as well as in the area of counseling and therapy.

BE PREPARED FOR THE MEETING

The evaluation discussion will be more fruitful when both parties are prepared. Prior to the meeting, they can, individually, review the previous period and bring supporting data with them. Both the superior and subordinate should make a list of items to be discussed at the meeting. This will expedite the meeting and ensure that everything is covered.

It is, of course, worthwhile to arrange for quiet during the meeting. Constant interruptions will distract the superior and might lead the subordinate to believe that the subject of the meeting is not very important. In addition, both parties can give more complete attention to the performance review.

STATE THE PURPOSE OF THE INTERVIEW AND PUT THE SUBORDINATE AT EASE

Most subordinates who are coming to a performance review session are likely to experience a certain amount of anxiety. Anxiety and fear inhibit clear communication and increase the likelihood of the use of defense mechanisms. When the subordinate is fearful, he may be more concerned about the reactions of his supervisor to what is said in the discussion rather than the subject of it.

To create an atmosphere of ease, the interview should be treated as a mutual problem-solving discussion. If the superior can create a supportive environment, acting as a helper and not solely as a judge, the subordinate's anxiety may be lessened, reducing the possibility of defensiveness and facilitating communications.

Of course, simply beginning in a nonthreatening way may not be enough to alleviate completely the subordinate's anxiety about the situation. The subordinate's reaction to the situation will depend on his previous experiences with the superior. If in the past the superior has been accepting, sympathetic, fair, courteous, and not punishment minded, the atmosphere will be much more relaxed and the subordinate much less inhibited than if the superior, by his past actions, has acted in an overbearing, fear-inducing way. Past indications of coldness, lack of interest, arbitrariness, or unfairness will make communication quite difficult. Superiors of this type tend to be formalistic, restrained, and slow, making understanding more difficult to achieve. *It is important to remember that the day-to-day behavior of the superior with his subordinate will do more to set the tone and will be the primary determinant of quality of the interview than how the superior begins and where he sits.*

FACILITATE DISCUSSION OF THE SUBJECT

There are a number of ways to facilitate a more open discussion during the performance review. Some of these are suggested here.

LISTEN ACTIVELY.   One way to encourage another to talk about a subject is to listen in an active way. Show your interest in what he is saying by maintaining a general look of alertness. Look right at the person talking. Nod your head often. This may encourage conversation because it communicates to the other that you accept and are interested in what he has to say.

USE THE REFLECTIVE SUMMARY.   Every once in a while you can summarize what you believe to be the other person's perception of feelings about a particular situation. The "reflective summary" consists of questions directed back at the other party. Examples of reflective summary are

> You feel that your assistants are completely unreliable?
> You're afraid you are falling way behind technically?

This indicates that you have been listening; it enables you to determine your own understanding of what the other person is saying; it forces you to put yourself in the place of another and see things from his point of view; and it emphasizes the importance of feelings as determinants of behavior rather than what is "really true."

It is generally unwise to directly challenge the validity of the subordinate's feelings. This would no doubt elicit defensive behavior—an argument or at least a disagreement. The subordinate may become cautious and inhibited in the interview.

The reflective summary also shows the subordinate that you respect his ideas. One research study shows that interviewers who were most disliked were those who did not show respect for the persons being interviewed.

USE SILENCE.   There may be times when the subordinate may either be reluctant to discuss a particular topic any further or feel that he has adequately explained a point, especially if it is related to his esteem needs. If it is desirable that he talk more about the topic, silence and an interested look from the superior may bring pressure on the subordinate to talk. Few individuals can tolerate a period of silence with another person, and most will feel a strong urge to talk under such conditions.

REWARD INSIGHT AND SELF-CRITICISM.   Individuals react to facial gestures, such as smiles and frowns, at appropriate places. Expressed opinions and thoughts that are met by signs of displeasure in the listener decrease in frequency. The expression of opinions and thoughts that meet with signs of acceptance and interest increase in frequency.

Actually, any person influences the verbal behavior of another unintentionally just by showing signs of acceptance or rejection of what is said. Although, for example, it is difficult for a person to be self-critical because of his self-esteem needs and the defense mechanisms that protect them, self-criticism may be a prerequisite of performance improvement. Consequently, the superior should show very active acceptance of self-critical behavior by smiling and nodding appropriately and show lack of acceptance of defensive behavior, such as the refusal to accept any blame for failure or false accusations against others, by frowning or other signs of displeasure. This approach does, however, require that the other person himself make the initial movement toward greater self-insight. It is this initial movement that is reinforced by the facial expressions.

BE HONEST IN YOUR ANSWERS.   The superior, because of his higher status, is most influential in setting the tone of the interview. If he is open, natural, and honest, then this helps develop similar subordinate behavior. Evasive answers from the superior create subordinate insecurity and doubt. Direct answers from the interviewer reduce anxiety.[1]

MINIMIZE CRITICISM.   To suggest that criticism should be minimized does not mean that it should be eliminated completely. The subordinate must know when the superior is not satisfied with progress. This information may be a necessary prerequisite of performance improvement.

Criticism is probably more important to some groups than others. We found, in the research described in Chapters 2 and 3, that an increase in criticism was related to greater effort expenditures for managers low in self-assurance and in those who saw a clear relationship between performing well and the receiving of organizational rewards, such as pay increases and advancements.* Of course, even among these groups, there might have been considerable defensive behavior at the time the criticism was given.

Criticisms may evoke defensive behavior from the subordinate,

---

* It should be noted here that increased effort does not necessarily mean better performance.

which may, in turn, generate defensiveness on the part of the boss. If the validity of the criticism is rejected, the superior may become defensive because his judgment is being criticized. A mutually defensive atmosphere might well lead to argument and disagreement, and worsen relations between the two men.

The negative effects of criticism were shown clearly in a research project at General Electric.[2] In this study, regularly scheduled appraisal interviews of exempt personnel were observed and then before-and-after measures of performance taken. The researchers found the following:

1. The average subordinate acted defensively to 54 per cent of his boss's criticisms.
2. Constructive responses to criticism rarely occurred (much less than one per interview).
3. In cases with *an above average amount* of criticism, the subordinate exhibited five times as much defensive behavior than the cases with an *average amount* of criticism.
4. Those that got an above average amount of criticism showed less favorable performance ten to twelve weeks later (and there was no evidence to support that they were generally poor performers).
5. Frequent criticism constituted so strong a threat to self-esteem that it disrupted performance.
6. There was more improved performance in less criticized areas than in the most criticized area.

In place of specific personal criticism, it is better to direct the discussion to the goals and the problems in achieving them. This enables the negative feedback to maintain an impersonal air, which is generally less threatening. Although lack of goal accomplishment may be threatening and elicit some defensive behavior, this should be reduced when the discussion is problem oriented rather than person oriented. For example, if the superior says "How can I help with the problems involved with the lag on the Burton project?" instead of saying "Why are you falling down on the Burton job?" he is likely to have a more effective review session.

ALLOW CATHARSIS IF FRUSTRATION IS PRESENT. Frustration arises when an individual is blocked from reaching a goal or achieving a result. Frustration is likely to be higher when

1. The person is close to goal accomplishment.
2. The goal is very important to him.

3. He did not expect to be blocked.
4. There are no perceived alternative goals or means to goals.

A frustrated subordinate might become quite emotionally upset during the goal review. When this happens, the best strategy is to allow the person to express his anger, which may reduce the state of tension. Catharsis means a draining away by allowing a frustrated person to express his anger freely. Often when a frustrated person can express anger without being subjected to criticism and attack, he can rid himself of his strong emotions; he will then perhaps be able to look at the problem objectively.

USE PROBING QUESTIONS. Formulating questions in such a way that the subordinate is forced to think of solutions, to evaluate solutions more fully, or to probe more deeply into the causes of problems is an important part of the review process. For instance, a manager might begin with

> Well, what do you think can be done about that?
> Are there any negative aspects of that solution?
> Could that problem by itself account for the results we got in the test run?
> You say he's too cautious—why might he behave that way?

Asking the right questions is one of the most important ways to develop real insight in the subordinate.

LIST DISAGREEMENTS

If possible, disagreements should be resolved before the goal review is ended. If not, both parties are liable to come away from the session frustrated, feeling a lack of accomplishment and a sense of incompleteness. Sometimes disagreement about progress or the causes of problems cannot be resolved unless more data or information is obtained. When this is the case, perhaps an assignment involving the collection of such information may serve as the logical end of the interview.

CLOSE THE REVIEW WITH A SUMMARY AND A PLAN

Ask the subordinate if everything that he wanted to talk about was discussed. Some research has indicated that interviews are considered successful by its participants if the needs of both parties are met.

The superior should summarize what the pair has agreed upon. This will make it more likely that both individuals come away from the review with a common understanding and set of expectations. In addition, a plan for resolving problems discovered should be formulated. Unless such plans are developed, the time and energy expended on identifying problems and ascertaining their causes will be wasted.

At this point, the manager must exercise extreme care not to appear to be imposing constraints on the subordinate that were never dealt with in the interview. Therefore, it seems extremely important to have summaries and plans that deal with what has gone on earlier in the discussion.

CARRYING OUT THE INTERMEDIATE REVIEW

A great deal of research on feedback indicates its significance in improving performance. Thus frequent intermediate review for MBO seems to be a worthwhile and important function. In the study of the MBO program discussed in Chapters 2 and 3, it was found that the more frequent the review of performance by the boss,

1. The more positive the feelings toward the MBO program.
2. The greater the goal success.
3. The greater the improvement in relations with the boss.
4. The clearer the goals appeared to be.
5. The more time the boss was thought to be spending on the MBO program.
6. The more it was perceived that the company had a strong interest in the MBO program.
7. The greater the satisfaction with the boss.
8. The more influence the subordinate felt he had on decisions made by his boss.
9. The more he viewed his boss as being helpful and concerned about him as an individual.

These results are not surprising. The amount of interaction is related to the quantity of feedback about performance and the nature of the goals involved. It can also be perceived as an indication of the superior's concern for the subordinate's performance.

In addition, it could be argued that more frequent review could lead to higher goal success because obstacles to goal accomplishment could be identified at an early stage.

We do not mean to imply from this research that there is no limit to the amount of time that a superior spends in performance review of his subordinates. As a matter of fact, if the supervisor spends too much time and attention on the performance of subordinates, it may be resented by them.

REVIEW CHARACTERISTICS AND TYPES OF SUBORDINATES

Our research suggests that the personality and perceptions of the subordinate influence his reactions to the review process. For example, more frequent performance review was related to higher goal accomplishment for those managers scoring low—but not for those scoring high—on the self-assurance subscale.* Thus it appears that, whereas managers high in self-assurance do not need the reinforcement, support, and feedback of the intermediate goal review to successfully accomplish goals, those managers with lower degrees of self-assurance do need this review.

The findings also suggest that more frequent review was related to more positive results (1) among managers in jobs with a high degree of changes, (2) among those who are lower on supervisory ability, and (3) among those who do not see a relationship between their performance and the reward system from the organization. The results of our study also support the notion that frequent review may be especially beneficial to managers with lower abilities, lower self-confidence, and lower levels of motivation.

MANAGEMENT TIME-ALLOCATION PROBLEMS

A manager's time is a scarce commodity. If he finds himself with too little time to carry out the intermediate goal review, some change in job duties must be made to provide it. A managerial time analysis, in which the individual keeps track of the time spent on his activities both by him alone and by others helping him may be one approach to finding this time. This could be done in at least two ways. A continuous activity log could be maintained for a certain period by the manager or by his secretary. Or, a work-sampling study could be carried out. Work sampling involves taking observations of work activity at random times instead of on a continuous basis and is less time-consuming than a continuous log of activities. Regardless of which method is used, when the data is collected, the manager must analyze his activities and determine which can be changed, delegated, or performed differently to gain more time for coaching and review.

* See Appendix B, the second article.

THE QUALITY OF THE SUBORDINATES

The time consumed in intermediate goal review is obviously going to vary with the quality of the subordinates and the nature of their goals. The greater the discrepancy between goal difficulty and the abilities of the subordinates, the more likely it is that problems will emerge and that the time required for the review function will increase. To alleviate this problem, attention should be given to matching the difficulty of goals with abilities. And because the abilities of subordinates are likely to vary, the superior will need more time with the less effective subordinates. This could cause problems if the other, more competent, managers feel that they are being neglected. To preclude this problem, the frequency of contact could be kept about the same for all subordinates, but the duration of contact could be much longer for those managers who need more help.

THE SUPERIOR'S MANNER

It is important to remember that during the intermediate goal review, problems should be identified early. As we have said, there is a natural tendency for individuals to be reluctant in admitting errors that might cause the boss to think less of them. Therefore, it is especially important during the intermediate goal review that the superior be open, warm, sympathetic, and non-critical. This type of behavior can go a long way in reducing fear and anxiety about admitting error. If the superior allows time pressures to force him to adopt an impatient or intolerant manner, early problem identification may be hindered.

THE UNDERESTIMATION OF TIME REQUIREMENTS

There is a tendency, especially by inexperienced personnel, to underestimate the time requirements of activities and programs. The boss should question time estimates of important projects, unless the subordinate has a reasonably good record of meeting schedules.

A primary reason for underestimating time requirements is the failure to anticipate contingencies. The inexperienced manager may assume there will be little or no interference with his work. The superior, by asking the right probing questions, can perhaps force the inclusion of contingencies in the time estimates of the subordinate. For example he can ask: "Okay, now give me an estimate based on the fact that you will get a couple of late deliveries?" or "Are you assuming that everyone else is going to get his job done on time?" or "What problems may come up to prevent you from achieving that schedule and how probable are they?"

DIFFICULTIES IN MEASUREMENT

To the extent that good criteria have been established in goal setting, the time requirements for the review process will be lessened. Target dates are especially useful here. If beginning and ending dates are assigned for each step in a program, it is a much simpler matter to evaluate the progress of the project.

If the goals involve largely routine work activities that generally focus on maintaining the present organization rather than advancing it, the evaluation may again be fairly simple. It may be nothing more than ascertaining whether or not an activity was completed and if it fell within acceptable tolerance limits. This argues for careful planning procedures and an organizational system characterized by clear policy, standard methods, standard procedures, and standard times. These facilitate the conduct of the review function.

Unusual, nonroutine, and self-development goals are harder to evaluate. As indicated in the chapter on goal setting, the evaluation of these goals would often be to determine if the action plan has been carried out.

RELATIVE PRESSURES OF ROUTINE VERSUS NONROUTINE ACTIVITIES

Routine, daily job activities of an individual create the primary time pressures to which he responds. They are immediate and generally demand a great deal of attention. Superiors must be aware of these demands on subordinates. Efforts should be made to see that these demands do not keep him from procrastinating on long term, nonroutine, but important projects.

This can be somewhat resolved by breaking down the major project into steps. Review of these steps can then be used as a means to ensure completion of the activity.

DEALING WITH FUNCTIONAL INTERDEPENDENCY

One may be unable to complete an assignment or program as scheduled because prerequisite activities have not been performed completely or appropriately by other managers or organizational units. When a subordinate encounters this type of difficulty, the superior must use his influence to overcome the difficulty and solve the problem. He may change the deadline, the goal, or change the action plan designed to accomplish the goal. Changing the goal would probably be the least desirable alternative because, if the goal was originally important, it probably still is. The most likely solution would be to alter completion dates. When this happens, it might be worthwhile to add a short-term project to the subordinate's goal assignments to replace the postponed goal. This might discourage the subordinate's trying to escape responsibility for goal accomplishment by failing to pressure other parts of the organization to perform their prerequisite activities on time.

Perhaps another method of achieving the goal could be adopted. Most objectives can be accomplished in several ways. This is especially true for goals dealing with changes in revenues, costs, or efficiency measures. As indicated previously, what was once the best means to an end, all factors considered, might turn out to be second or even fifth best when scheduling difficulties are encountered.

THE FINAL GOAL REVIEW

Generally, the final goal review involves the final determination of a goal accomplishment rather than progress toward the completion of a goal. However, this may not be the case when goals have a longer time span than the one year typically designated for goal accomplishment. In such cases, a progress review is the only thing possible. Personal development goals are especially likely to fall in this category, but sometimes the activities engaged in to accomplish the personal development goal consist of a series of unique events that could be evaluated on the basis of completion or noncompletion of the event.

Defensiveness may be more of a problem in the final review than in the intermediate review, since the subordinate recognizes that it is a time of general summing up of performance. This defensiveness may be minimized if the orientation of the final goal review is on future problems and their solutions. By emphasizing the support that a superior can give, or new ways of doing things, rather than criticism for errors and mistakes, some of the defensiveness may be reduced.

EVALUATING GOAL ACCOMPLISHMENT

Difficulties in evaluating over-all goal accomplishment increase with the number of goals, the degree of variability of subordinate's accomplishment, variation in goal importance, and the different possible causes of goal failure.

Each goal must be considered as well as the degree to which it was accomplished. As indicated previously, if the goal is exceeded, this too should be indicated. For example, a goal can be described as having been accomplished at the 120 per cent level.

DEADLINES AND TIME LIMITATIONS

Typically, different goals have different designated completion dates. It is important not only that the goal be accomplished but that it be accomplished on time. Designated completion dates are obviously most important when work is interdependent. If a manager fails to achieve a given objective by a certain time, other managers or other organizations may be prevented from achieving their goals on time.

THE RELATIVE IMPORTANCE OF GOALS

When evaluating over-all goal accomplishment, it is important to keep in mind the relative importance of the various goals. A manager should have some sense of goal priority in his work. It might be far more worthwhile to accomplish a very important goal at 100 per cent than to make sure that relatively unimportant goals are met at 120 per cent.

MEANS OF REACHING GOALS

Some advocates of an objectives-oriented approach seem to assert that one should not care how results are achieved but only whether they are achieved. This is a patently foolish position to take. The means to goal achievement are important and should be considered. If the means used to reach goals generate dysfunctional consequences for the organization or its components, little may be gained. Action plans of managers may result in lawsuits, impaired morale, loss of personnel through resignations, or increase in interdepartmental conflict. Obviously, any results obtained should be worth their costs. Thus, it would be wise to put at least a subjective value on such things as morale and cooperation in calculating such costs.

It should also be noted when the means used to reach certain ends are creative, or have positive by-products, such as improvements in the development of organizational personnel, higher morale, or more efficient use of resources. These are values generated by an individual that should be rewarded in some form or other.

DETERMINING THE CAUSES OF LACK OF GOAL ACCOMPLISHMENT

In the final goal review, it is very important to correctly ascertain the reasons for failure. Did the performance deficiencies lie in the capabilities of the subordinate himself? Was the failure a result of factors beyond his control, such as a change in the organization's plans, nondelivery of required parts, budgetary cuts? Did failure arise because of accident or illnesses? It is important to make as precise a determination as possible in cases of failures because the circumstances surrounding the manager's failure may not be as obvious in the future when a manager's personnel record is examined. It is important not to penalize an individual for events that are beyond his control. This can only lead to a loss of faith in the system, to low morale, and to diminished motivation.

If on the other hand, the lack of goal accomplishment was due to some personal deficiency, this should be noted. Those deficiencies that are correctable through training and development should become the personal development goals for that subordinate in the next goal-setting period.

THE AVOIDANCE OF A SENSE OF FAILURE

Where possible, every effort should be made to ensure that the subordinate comes away from the final goal review with a sense of success. Previous research has indicated that a feeling of competence is related to higher performance in subsequent periods, and a feeling of failure is often followed by lower levels of aspiration and motivation.[3] To avoid the sense of failure the superior must not concentrate on failures. He must talk about the successes achieved.

SELF-REVIEW AND THE ACCEPTANCE OF DEFICIENCIES

Research conducted at General Electric indicated that when subordinates prepared their own performance appraisals there was less defensive behavior and more satisfaction than under a more traditional appraisal program in which subordinates were told their weaknesses by their superiors.[4] In addition, subsequent performance for the self-review group was higher. Other research on the subject also shows that self-ratings may be valuable in this regard.[5] Perhaps positive results would ensue if the superior were to ask the subordinate to identify his own personal deficiencies before the final goal review. This self-evaluation could form the basis for discussion of new personal development goals.

SUMMARY

The manner in which the review process is carried out is of critical importance to the success of the MBO program as a whole. Our research indicates its importance. Feedback frequency was significantly related to attitudes both toward the MBO program and toward the superior. The review process seems to be especially important for managers who are lower in ability, lack confidence, and are operating at lower motivational levels.

The critical elements in the review process seem to be the amount of effort expended on it and the interpersonal communications skills of the superior when communicating with subordinates. Perhaps the time available for the review process could be increased by a more efficient allocation of managerial work activities. The time required for conducting the sessions can be reduced with better planning, the use of performance standards and controls, and a systematic approach to MBO.

The interpersonal skills of the superior can be increased through the acquisition of additional knowledge in human relations, by training in carrying out review sessions (the role-playing method seems to be most effective for this), and by a constant self-evaluation of one's interpersonal behavior. Each time a review session occurs, one should evaluate it immediately. One might ask himself: What went well? What went badly? Why? What should I do differently next time? and so on. In general, any improvements in the way that the review is conducted should be beneficial to the effectiveness of the MBO program.

NOTES

1. Carroll, S. J., Jr., and A. N. Nash. *The Evaluation of Performance*. Mimeographed manuscript. College Park, Md.: University of Maryland, Book Store, 1970.
2. Meyer, H. H., E. Kay, and J. R. P. French. "Split Roles in Performance Appraisal," *Harvard Business Review*, 43 (1965), 123–129.
3. Korman, A. K. "A Consistency Model of Work Behavior," Symposium on Theoretical Developments in Industrial Psychology. *American Psychological Association, Annual Meetings*, San Francisco, Calif., 1968.
4. Bassett, G. A., and H. H. Meyer. "Performance Appraisal Based on Self-review," *Personnel Psychology*, 21 (1968), 421–430.
5. Barrett, R. *Performance Rating*. Chicago: Science Research Associates, 1966.

6
INTEGRATING MBO WITH OTHER SYSTEMS

In his study of the failure of MBO in an English factory, Wickens pointed out that one important reason for this was because the program was not institutionalized.[1] Unless the MBO program is integrated with other organizational procedures and systems, it will be viewed as something outside normal operating procedure and will receive inadequate attention. In addition, it will create a source of conflict, as it is likely that action required by the MBO program will contradict other procedures and requirements. Also, unless the various organizational systems are tied into MBO, it will be very difficult to carry out the MBO process. Market forecasts must be available for goal setting, for example. The data-processing system must provide data on such factors as costs, revenues, waste, down time, units produced, deliveries, man-power hours, and new orders, in the right form and at the right time to periodically evaluate the goal progress of the organization's managerial personnel.

The more that the MBO system is made interdependent with other subsystems of the organization, the more the use of MBO will be reinforced and will become a natural aspect of management. However, there are many problems in integrating the MBO program with other organizational systems, in that changes must often be made in these subsystems. In this chapter, we shall discuss some of these problems and various approaches for resolving them.

THE BUDGETING PROCESS

Anthony defines budgeting as a

> process of planning the overall activity of the enterprise for a specified period of time, usually a year. An important objective of this process is to fit together the separate plans made for various segments of the enterprise so as to assure that these plans harmonize with one another and that the aggregate effect of all of them on the whole enterprise is satisfactory.[2]

The company budget is composed of several major parts. The marketing budget generally includes both projected sales levels and selling expenses. The manufacturing budget may detail factory operating costs, such as materials, overhead, and labor. Administrative budgets are projected costs for general management and administrative expenses. Research and development activities are likely to be expressed in a separate budget.

These budgets are important documents for the objectives process, as the projected activity and expense levels may be used in the development of goal statements. Sales budget estimates, for example, serve as the basis for the formulation and realization of action plans. Budgeted expenditures represent commitments of resources that management is willing to expend in particular units or on specific projects to achieve desired goals. These commitments provide a basis for developing and implementing action plans at all levels of the organization. The general relationship between the budget and MBO is obvious and need not be belabored. Yet there are some general points that may present a problem when integrating the budget and MBO. These are

1. Translating budget data into departmental requirements and objectives.
2. The amount of subordinate participation.
3. The timing problems of integrating MBO and budgets.

TRANSLATING BUDGETS INTO GOAL STATEMENTS

Budget constraints are translated into operating plans at each level; that is, general figures are broken down into specific projects. These product-line budget estimates may be further defined as unit or individual quotas, or projected activity levels for particular geographic areas.

Translating general budget requirements into specific ones is simple enough within a particular department. It is a factoring of the general costs or revenues into components associated with a particular unit. These figures can be used as performance goals for the major departmental activities and for deriving goal statements for supporting units. Once it is known, for example, that 10,000 product units is the budgeted sales level, certain types and levels of sales promotion and other support activity may be required to achieve the desired sales. Managers responsible for these support and facilitating activities can use the budget sales estimate for construction of action plans that directly support the marketing efforts to achieve the sales goal. The goal may be expressed as completion of a particular project by a specific target date.

It is in this same manner that general organizational budgets are translated into different departmental requirements. For instance, let us assume that the master budget for the organization is stated in expected sales revenue and operating costs. First, the sales volume must be broken down by product line and by period. The marketing department may use these data, as suggested above, to develop performance goals. The manufacturing division must translate the market requirements, as stated in the sales budgets, into manufacturing activities and projects. For example, production lead times and manpower costs are important considerations in the goal-setting processes in manufacturing. Production schedules must be set, from which manpower requirements are then determined. In addition, goal statements at the highest organization level must be stated in terms and concepts meaningful to the manufacturing function. Whereas "sales volume per employee" may be an appropriate aggregate measure, "production cost per production employee" may be a more relevant goal for the manufacturing manager, and therefore should be used. This can then be translated into something meaningful for lower manufacturing personnel.

The budget is relatively easy to translate into operational requirements for manufacturing and marketing functions. It is more difficult for technical and support staffs, especially for the engineering and research segments. Generally, these units must translate the budget into project plans. But because projects may not conform with the regular activity cycle of the firm, it becomes difficult to match a periodic budget with specific sums for a set of projects, the results of which will probably not be realized within the budget period, or perhaps for several years thereafter. Management decisions must be made, possibly with great subjectivity, as to the allocation of dollars among the projects.

The measurement problem is most difficult in these cases. Goal achievement should be assessed in terms of whether specific phases of the project have been completed or project costs have been met. This, of course, will not ensure that the project, when finally completed, will be successful in the plant or the market place. However, the value is assumed to be adequate when a decision is made by higher-management levels to proceed with the projects. Thus, research and engineering staffs, as well as other staff functions, should be concerned with meeting time and dollar deadlines within certain quality constraints.

THE TIMING PROBLEM

It is indeed a difficult coordination task simply to prepare and disseminate the budget. Three months or more lead time may be required from the date when information and data collection begin until the time the final document is operational.

But an additional set of problems must be faced when MBO is integrated with the budgeting progress. Budgets are prepared and filtered through the organization *before the results of the previous operating period are final.* Therefore, the budget preparation and dissemination period may best be used for setting performance objectives rather than for performance reviews—because of the unavailability of the results of the previous period. Thus, the nature and timing of the budget process is such that performance goal setting and performance review must be separated in time. The first meeting, held during the budget preparation and dissemination period emphasizes setting performance goals. A later meeting, held after the results of the previous period are available, would be appropriate for performance review and setting self-improvement goals for the forthcoming period.

These relationships are illustrated more specifically in Figure 6–1. Consider A, B, C, and D to be operating periods for which budgets are prepared. A budget for A will be prepared prior to the period. When it is completed, the chief executive can use it to set performance goals for executives of each major division. They, in turn, can translate these into action plans and activities for their subordinates, and so on down the line. The degree of interaction and subordinate involvement at lower organizational levels is a function of the extent to which the objectives approach is implemented. At any rate, up to this point in time, only performance goals should be set. These are goals that can be drawn from the budget.

FIGURE 6–1   TIMING OF GOAL-SETTING AND PERFORMANCE-REVIEW SESSIONS

Budget A		Budget B	Budget C	Budget D
Performance Goal Setting for A		Performance Goal Setting for B	Performance Goal Setting for C	Performance Goal Setting for D
	Operating Period A	Operating Period B	Operating Period C	Operating Period D
	Results Previous Period	Results A	Results B	Results C
	Personal Goal Setting for A	Performance and Personal Goal Evaluation A	Performance and Personal Goal Evaluation B	Performance and Personal Goal Evaluation C
	Results Evaluation	Personal Goal Setting for B	Personal Goal Setting for C	Personal Goal Setting for D

The results of the preceding operating period will not be available until *after* A has begun. These results should reflect the attainment of performance goals for the previous period and will be the criteria for evaluation of performance of the responsible executives. When they become available, a meeting between superior and subordinate should be scheduled to review them. This meeting is an evaluation interview at which performance is appraised. Reasons for failure to achieve goals should be sought, if performance has been inadequate. This appraisal provides a springboard for discussion and determination of individual self-improvement and development goals. At this meeting, the emphasis is on performance evaluation and setting personal improvement, or developmental, goals for the forthcoming period.

Of course, near the end of period A, the budget for period B will be constructed. During this process, performance goals should be worked out for the forthcoming period B. When the results for period A become available, an evaluation session should be scheduled, during period B, to review the achievement of performance goals for A and to set self-improvement and development goals.

Some of our earlier data suggest that where the attempt was made to conduct both goal setting and performance review in one session, the review process was slighted.[3] In our interview study, managers were fairly satisfied with the planning and goal-setting process but did not believe that they received adequate feedback and review.

The timing sequence suggested here has to do with major goal-setting and review meetings. It is not meant to imply that they be the only superior–subordinate interactions that deal with performance and feedback. Other discussions about operating results, during which feedback is given, should be held frequently. The goals developed in the objectives process should be the basis of these discussions, too.

SUBORDINATE PARTICIPATION

The degree of involvement, influence, and participation of subordinates is a question that must be treated. The budget, by its very nature, sets constraints. It describes activity levels, such as sales volume or production quantities, desired by higher-level management. To the extent that these are relatively fixed or rigid, the nature and type of participation is limited.

It is highly unlikely that managers at higher levels will allow a great deal of subordinate influence in determination of goal levels. When this is the case, subordinate participation in the budgeting and goal-setting process should primarily be oriented toward *how* to achieve the goal levels. In other words, instead of determining how much should be achieved, subordinates should be extremely involved in the development of action plans to achieve those goals. Other factors such as subordinate competence, organizational level, and the criticality of the situation must also be taken into consideration, however.

PERFORMANCE APPRAISAL

MBO is most commonly viewed as an alternative method of performance appraisal. Other evaluation techniques have been criticized for failing to relate individual performance ratings to results. MBO is generally considered a method that emphasizes performance results and not subjective factors, which are at best only indirectly related to output.

Performance appraisal has two major purposes. The first is to evaluate the quality of performance in the present assignment by pinpointing those areas in which an individual has performed well and those in which requirements have not been met. This examination provides both parties in the evaluation with a basis for determining what might be done to improve performance. Current performance may also be evaluated to determine the amount of compensation increase that an individual should receive.

The second major function of performance appraisal is the identification of management potential. Higher-level positions should be filled by those who are most qualified, but the determination of higher-level qualifications is another matter, as we shall see.

Given the many purposes of appraisal methods, it is little wonder that a single method may not be adequate.[4] One approach should evaluate performance, another may be required to estimate potential, a third variant may be needed for coaching and counseling, and a final one for the determination of compensation increases. These need not be independent systems, in that they might all make use of the same data. However, the data might be used in different ways and different conclusions drawn from it, depending on the type of personnel decision to be made.

In addition to these problems, bias on the part of the rater and the development of good criteria also compound the difficulties typically found in performance rating.[5] Ratings based on personality traits seem especially susceptible to rater bias.

Some resolution of these problems may be achieved with the objectives approach. The use of results as evaluation criteria makes it possible to avoid the use of indirect, nebulous personality traits. A goal was achieved or it was not. An action plan was carried out or it was not. The reasons for success and failure can be sought with these more objective criteria as a base. The evaluator is able to provide feedback based on performance-relevant characteristics. He can focus upon problems resulting primarily from performance rather than personality deficiencies. The criteria should be perceived as more relevant, clear, and meaningful by the subordinate, as he should be more aware of the relationship of goals and objectives of his performance.

THE IDENTIFICATION OF MANAGEMENT POTENTIAL

MBO can be regarded as a reasonably effective method of evaluating current performance and a sound basis for coaching and counseling, but it may be limited as a means for the assessment of potential. Although it may be that past performance is the best predictor of future performance, there are other factors that should be taken into account. Accomplishment of goals in the present position may be a good indicator of capability in that position, or of general motivation, but not of abilities to perform at a higher level of responsibilities especially if the requirements are logical extensions of activities in other positions in which the individual has been unsuccessful.

In any event, something other than ability to perform on the present job must be evaluated. The individual's capacity to adjust and function in different situations must also be considered along with his potential ability for different job situations. It may be that this aspect is best evaluated by the traditional trait or characteristic approach. Certainly, such an evaluation should be carefully made, perhaps by a group of higher-level managers. At any rate, this type of evaluation supplement to MBO is necessary in any organization, and the MBO program in itself cannot serve as the only means of appraising performance in an organization.

MANAGEMENT DEVELOPMENT

MBO can be an important complement to formal management development efforts. Management development has been defined by House as

> any attempt to improve current or future managerial performances by imparting information, conditioning attitudes or increasing skills. Hence, management development includes such efforts as on-the-job coaching, counseling, classroom training, job rotation, selected readings, planned experience, and assignment to understudy positions.[6]

Development efforts may be grouped into two general categories. On-the-job efforts are those that take place in the day-to-day working environment. These include techniques such as job rotation, performance appraisal, and coaching. Off-the-job development efforts are those that take place in a setting away from the place of work, essentially in classrooms or laboratories.

MBO can be used to support and reinforce both types of development. It can, and should, be considered a developmental method in its own right. It embodies coaching, performance appraisal, and feedback and counseling. It occurs within the context of the job environment. In addition, the content of off-the-job development techniques can be reinforced with MBO. The objectives approach can thus be an important adjunct to other methods.

MBO AS A COMPLEMENT TO OTHER METHODS

MBO can reinforce off-the-job development efforts. One of the major problems that has precipitated disenchantment with executive training and development is that the environmental conditions to which a trainee returns are such that there is little or no reinforcement of the learning that has taken place in the classroom. The place of work is of such a nature that what is learned is either inappropriate when applied to it, or if appropriate, meets either with no support or even with negative reinforcement from the system.

This problem can be somewhat alleviated by MBO. By developing goal statements derived from the content of the development effort, and using them as part of the objectives approach, trained managers will be more cognizant of what part of management development is relevant to the job. If there is any mutual goal setting at all, the subordinate can take the initiative and propose goals that utilize training content and thereby open the discussion of its relevance with the superior. Together they can direct attention to areas and concepts that are useful on the job and can work out methods and plans for implementing and measuring these.

Obviously, goals of this nature would be appropriate only for those who have been exposed to some training or developmental effort. If this type of goal is set, it is important that the superior be knowledgeable about the training content and job application. This, in and of itself, may be a positive benefit to the reinforcement of development.

We have discussed how MBO can complement a formal training program that has already occurred. It can also be used as the basis for such a training program. Carroll and Nash, in a study of reactions to a formal management development program for first-line supervisors, found that reactions to such a program were more favorable when the program dealt with job problems of current concern to the participants, and when they saw a relationship between using the training and obtaining various types of rewards corresponding to their interests and goals.[7] Based on these results, a training program that is made relevant to the goals that the participants currently have or that focuses on causes of failure to achieve past goals should be reacted to favorably by participants.

MBO AS A DEVELOPMENTAL METHOD

The MBO approach can be used itself as a very effective development method. Any regular job-focused goal with feedback provides development. However, goals can be established for subordinates in such a way that they provide a specific learning experience for them. In other words, goals can be tailored to the deficiencies of the individual. Obviously this will contradict a previously stated suggestion that goals be established in such a way as to draw upon an individual's unique strengths in terms of knowledge or skill. However, it is recommended that only one or a very few of a subordinate's goals be used to make up deficiencies. An example of such a developmental goal assignment would be to have a personnel manager weak on knowledge of the field of wage and salary administration evaluate the organization's wage and salary program. This assignment would require him to learn something about the subject. In addition to the special-project type of goal, several company MBO programs provide for the use of personal development goals along with job goals. Such personal development goals, as indicated previously, probably provide most motivation for self-development when they focus on causes for lack of accomplishment of assigned job goals and when they are accepted as real deficiencies by the individual involved.

USING MBO TO IMPROVE PERFORMANCE THROUGH FEEDBACK

As indicated earlier, regularly scheduled feedback sessions are necessary in an MBO program. Many managers would argue that they are constantly appraising performance and providing feedback and that their subordinates always know where they stand. These managers assume that all interactions with subordinates is feedback. Although it is no doubt true that the subordinate may be frequently interpreting superior behavior evaluatively, he may not respond in the manner intended by the boss. The subordinate may have little or no reason to believe that there is anything wrong with his current performance and thus reject ambiguous or negative cues. In discriminating between positive and negative signals in the environment, he may select those cues or stimuli consistent with his perception that his performance is adequate. For this reason, it seems best to provide a specific situation where performance is to be discussed. It will then be clear to both the superior and the subordinate that both successful and unsuccessful performance are to be examined at this time.

The feedback interview itself is important in the performance of the coaching function. Unless there is something drastically wrong with the subordinate's performance that could lead to possible removal from his position, the meeting should be directed at seeking methods for improvement of performance. What can the subordinate do? How can he reorganize his activities to meet objectives? Are his perceptions of the job and the boss's expectations clear? This approach places the emphasis not on criticism but on resolving problems and leads naturally to the opportunity to set personal improvement and development goals. Little time will need to be taken up with setting new job goals, which will have been set already during the budget preparation period, so the emphasis can be on performance review and developmental goal setting.

COMPENSATION

As indicated previously, some research studies indicate that individuals who perceive that performance is related to the reward system perform at a higher level.[8] In our study, we found that this held true only when goals were difficult.* In addition, we found that criticism from the boss was associated with higher effort expenditures among managers who believed that performance was related to the reward system but that there was no such association among managers who did not believe that performance was related to rewards.† We also found that a perception that pay was related to performance level correlated significantly with higher satisfaction with pay, with higher satisfaction with the boss, with higher satisfaction with the job, with a perception that the boss would be very concerned with the subordinate's goal failure, and with a more positive attitude toward the MBO approach as a whole.‡ An unpublished study by a student of one of the authors found a relationship, although small, between perceptions of a relationship between performance and the reward system and actual performance ratings.** Carroll and Nash found strong perceptions of a relationship between performance and rewards significantly related to plans to use management training on the job.[9]

In spite of the evidence that the performance level does seem to be higher when managers see a relationship between performance and the reward system, a number of studies show very little relationship between salary and performance ratings, even when the managerial level is held constant.[10] What are the opinions of managers themselves with respect to this issue? Lawler has cited two studies that indicated that managers, especially the better educated, prefer to have their pay based on performance or merit.[11] Thus, the research evidence cited has indicated that performance is likely to be higher when managers see a relationship between performance and the reward system and that managers believe that rewards should be based on merit; yet there appears to be only a slight relationship between rated performance and salaries received.

On the basis of his review of the research on this topic, Lawler concludes that the best pay plan in terms of providing the most motivation to perform at a higher level would be a system of MBO tied to the salary system. He proposes specifically that at the beginning of the year the

> superior and subordinate would jointly decide on three things. First, they would decide on the objectives the subordinate should try to achieve during the ensuing time period. Second, they would decide how the subordinate's progress toward these objectives will be

* See Appendix B, the first article.
† See Appendix B, the second article.
‡ The correlations here among perceiving a relationship between performance and pay and the other factors mentioned were $r = .51$ for satisfaction with pay, $r = .38$ for satisfaction with the boss, $r = .39$ for satisfaction with the job, $r = .28$ with perceived boss concern for goal failure, and $r = .22$ with positive attitude toward the MBO program.
** The correlation was $r = .23$ (biserial).

measured. . . . Third, they would decide what level of reward the subordinate would receive if he accomplishes his objectives.[12]

We think that it is probably not possible to specify in advance what rewards a man will receive if he achieves his goals. As we indicated earlier, it is a difficult process to assess goal accomplishment at the end of the year. It is likely for example, that some goals will have been changed to some extent and that there was deficient goal accomplishment on other goals for reasons beyond the subordinate's control. In addition, it is likely that some goals will have been achieved at more than 100 per cent and some at less than this figure. The priority or importance of the goals accomplished as well as their difficulty relative to those not accomplished must be considered. Also, as indicated earlier, the means used to accomplish goals must be evaluated. It is obviously of great importance that the organization not reward behavior that is unethical, illegal, or that creates future or other current problems for the organization. A manager might achieve his goals at the expense of creating ill will or future problems for the organization or by contributing to the nonaccomplishment of the goals of others. Another consideration is whether goals were routine or nonroutine goals. If the goals assigned to a manager are routine or normal job duty goals, then by accomplishing his goals the individual is simply carrying out his job.

Thus, compensation decisions based on performance under a MBO program must be made at the end of the period of goal accomplishment rather than before. However, we do agree with Lawler that performance under the MBO program should be related to the reward system and, furthermore, that salary decisions be based on the kinds of goals that were achieved.

Tying the reward system to MBO does not mean that salary decisions must be made and communicated during the final performance review period. Several organizations, including the one that we studied, found that discussing performance improvement and salaries at the very same time did not have good results.[13] The salary issue during such sessions tends to create so much emotional feeling that a rational and objective discussion of performance becomes very difficult if not impossible. Also, during the final performance review period, attention must be directed at determining why goals were or were not accomplished. It is an information-gathering period, and the superior in such a situation simply does not have the necessary information to make such an important decision as a salary decision at that time. Therefore, the salary decision should be made and communicated to the subordinate at a later session after all the facts about a subordinate's performance have been carefully evaluated. The subordinate should be called in and the salary decision should be communicated to him with an explanation of the basis on which it was made. The part of the salary increase that is attributed to goal accomplishment as compared to that which is given for other factors, such as cost-of-living increases or for gaining skills valuable to the organization in the future, should be made clear. Compensation decisions with respect to any supplementary compensation programs, such as stock options, bonus plans, or profit-sharing plans, should also be made and communicated at this time, as, typically, such compensation is supposed to be tied to performance.

MBO may *not* be particularly useful in setting basic compensation levels for particular positions. This requires more information than could be obtained using the objectives approach. External market considerations, such as salaries for similar jobs in other organizations, or the scarcity of individuals with particular skills, must come into play when determining base salary levels and ranges.

Internal wage administration may be facilitated with the objectives approach. MBO can be of assistance in developing salary differentials within a particular job class. By assessing the level of difficulty and contribution of goals for a particular job and comparing them with similar jobs in that class or that type, some determination of the appropriateness of basic compensation differentials can be made.

MBO can also be useful in providing information about changes in job requirements that may necessitate re-evaluation and adjustment of compensation levels for different positions. By observing changes in objectives over time, it may be possible to detect changes in job requirements that would lead to revisions in compensation schedules. A problem here needs to be noted, however. Because of an individual's initiative and aggressiveness, goals may be set that go substantially beyond the current job requirements. If this happens, the appropriate strategy may be to change the position of the individual rather than to redefine the job and make changes in compensation.

SUMMARY

The chapter stresses the importance of integrating MBO into the job of managing and relating it to other organizational processes and procedures. The discussion also indicates that the MBO process should especially be made congruent with the budgeting, performance appraisal, management development, and compensation programs. Problems of adapting the MBO approach to these programs are pointed out. By making MBO an integral part of management, managers will learn to use MBO in a natural manner, thereby achieving higher degrees of goal success.

NOTES

1. Wickens, J. D. "Management by Objectives: An Appraisal," *Journal of Management Studies,* **5** (1968), 365–379.
2. Anthony, R. *Managerial Accounting.* Homewood, Ill.: Irwin, 1960.
3. Tosi, H. L., Jr., and S. J. Carroll, Jr. "Managerial Reaction to Management by Objectives," *Academy of Management Journal,* **11** (1968), 415–426.
4. Barrett, R. *Performance Rating.* Chicago: Science Research Associates, 1966.
5. Barrett, 1966, op. cit.
6. House, R. *Management Development: Design, Evaluation and Implementation.* Ann Arbor, Mich.: Bureau of Industrial Relations, University of Michigan, 1967.
7. Carroll, S. J., Jr., and A. N. Nash. "Some Personal and Situational Correlates of Reactions to Management Development Training," *Academy of Management Journal,* **13** (1970), 187–196.
8. Georgopoulos, B. S., G. M. Mahoney, and M. N. W. Jones. "A Path Goal Approach to Productivity," *Journal of Applied Psychology,* **41** (1957), 345–353. Galbraith, J., and L. L. Cummings. "An Empirical Investigation of the Motivational Determinants of Task Performance: Interactive Effects Between Instrumentality-Valence and Motivation Ability," *Organizational Behavior and Human Performance,* **2** (1967), 237–357. Hackman, J. R., and L. W. Porter. "Expectancy Theory Predictions of Work Effectiveness," *Organizational Behavior and Human Performance,* **3** (1968), 417–426. Porter, L. W., and E. E. Lawler III. *Managerial Attitudes and Performance.* Homewood, Ill.: Irwin, 1968.
9. Carroll and Nash, 1970, op. cit.
10. Lawler, E. E. III. *Pay and Organizational Effectiveness.* New York: McGraw-Hill, 1971.
11. Lawler, 1971, op. cit.
12. Lawler, 1971, op. cit.
13. Preston, S. J. "J. Stone's Management by Objectives," *Personnel* (London) **1** (1968), 22–25. Meyer, H. H., E. Kay, and J. R. P. French, Jr. "Split Roles in Performance Appraisal," *Harvard Business Review,* **43** (1965), 123–239.

7
MBO—PRESENT AND FUTURE

This book has summarized most of the writing about the MBO approach. We have described our own research, that conducted by other investigators, the basic behavioral science research relevant to various aspects of this management approach, and the implications of this research for practice. In this section we attempt to draw some general conclusions about MBO, discuss its advantages and disadvantages, mention some future research needs, suggest some possible extensions of MBO to other groups, and make some predictions about the future.

THE EFFECTIVENESS OF MBO

The very limited research in this area makes it difficult to determine the cause–effect relationship of MBO and organization performance. Only one study has attempted to relate changes in the economic performance of the

121

organization to the installation of an MBO program. In this case the installation of the MBO program was followed by the reversal of a downward trend in over-all productivity.[1] However, this could have been simply a matter of coincidence. Productivity could rise and fall for any number of different reasons that may in no way be related to the installation of MBO. The organization where our research was conducted has also grown quite rapidly since the installation of the program. Here again, however, this growth might be related only slightly to the installation of MBO. What is needed is a more controlled experimental study in which MBO is introduced in an organization in certain divisions only. If such divisions were chosen randomly and if before-and-after measures of productivity were taken in both the experimental divisions where MBO was introduced and in the control divisions where MBO was not established, it would be possible to determine whether MBO does influence productivity.

MBO has a much clearer relationship to managerial attitudes and to the manner in which managers carry out their job assignments. As Raia in his first study at Purex concluded,

> A contribution of the program in the area of performance appraisal has been quite significant. There was unanimous agreement among the line managers in the department, particularly plant managers, [that] the Goals and Controls had simplified the evaluation of the individual's performance. The statement by the manager who, while being interviewed, remarked that he was now judged by his job performance and not "by the way I comb my hair," is quite meaningful.[2]

At General Electric, Meyer, Kay, and French compared GE managers using an MBO system to managers operating under the firm's traditional performance appraisal method.[3] They found that managers operating under the old appraisal method did not change their attitudes or behavior in the areas measured, whereas the managers operating under MBO indicated that their boss was giving them more help in improving performance on the job and in planning for future job opportunities, and was more receptive to new ideas. Those using MBO found planning to be easier and believed that better use was made of their abilities and experience. They also felt that the performance discussions with their boss were more valuable. Finally, members of the MBO group were more likely to have taken specific actions to improve performance than the managers operating under the traditional types of performance appraisal system.

Our study yielded similar results at Black & Decker. There, managers felt that MBO resulted in better and fairer appraisals of performance and that the MBO program did contribute to better planning, motivation, and communication.

However, the research indicates that MBO is not without its problems. Our research confirmed Raia's findings that managers using MBO believe that they are too busy with paper work and that the time demands of this approach are excessive. In addition, because the goals assigned to different individuals differ in complexity and difficulty, there is some feeling that the system may not be completely fair to different organizational members.

THE MBO PROCESS

As indicated in Chapters 1 and 4, the MBO process consists of the establishment of higher-level goals, the development of subordinate goals and action plans, the intermediate review of goal progress, and the final review of goal accomplishment. The research conducted at Black & Decker and reported in Chapters 2, 3, and 4 clearly indicates that various psychological and situational factors influence (1) the manner in which the MBO process is carried out, (2) the reactions to MBO by the superior and the subordinate, and (3) the results achieved under the program.

A SUMMARY OF RELATIONSHIPS IN THE MBO PROCESS

Figure 7–1 describes the interrelationships between the various aspects of the MBO process and is a model of the MBO process between individual superior–subordinate pairs. The model describes what we believe to be the most critical factors of the MBO process as identified through the various research studies we conducted.

PERSONAL, JOB, AND ORGANIZATIONAL CHARACTERISTICS

THE MBO APPROACH AT THE NEXT-HIGHER LEVEL. We found that the way in which the MBO process is carried out at the next-higher level is related to the goal-setting and performance review procedures used by individual managers. For example, as indicated earlier, there was a tendency for subordinates who received more frequent performance review from their superiors to give significantly more frequent performance review to managers reporting to them. Higher amounts of participation in goal setting for managers at one level were associated with higher amounts of participation

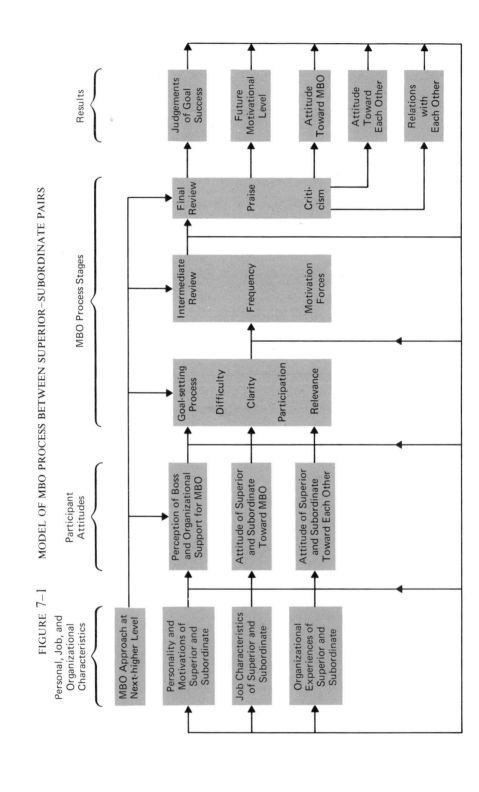

FIGURE 7-1   MODEL OF MBO PROCESS BETWEEN SUPERIOR–SUBORDINATE PAIRS

in goal setting for the subordinates of these managers. Clarity of goals and the establishment of priorities for goals at one level were associated with these same goal characteristics at the next-lower level. These findings suggest that superiors do serve as behavioral models for their subordinates, at least to some degree. It must be remembered, however, that these data were collected in the early stages of an MBO program. It is thus possible that modeling behavior is most pronounced when managers are uncertain as to the most appropriate behavior for the situation.

PERSONALITY AND MOTIVATIONS OF THE SUPERIOR AND THE SUBORDINATE. Our findings indicate that the personality and motivations of both the superior and the subordinate influence the manner in which the MBO process is carried out and the results attained under a particular MBO approach. One analysis of our data, for example, indicated that similarity in personality between the superior and subordinate was slightly related to the frequency of performance review. This is not surprising. We would expect that individuals who are similar would find it easier to interact than dissimilar individuals. Other analyses of the data indicated that superiors scoring higher on decisiveness and self-assurance on the Ghiselli Self-Description Inventory set more goals for subordinates, set goals that were greater in difficulty, allowed their subordinates more participation in the goal-setting process, set clearer goals, and provided more frequent performance review than managers who were scored as more cautious than decisive and who had lower self-assurance scores on the GSDI. These results are not unexpected. The more cautious manager with less self-assurance would probably have less confidence in the ability of his subordinates and perhaps also in his own ability to interact effectively with his subordinates, and this would be reflected in his approach to goal setting and performance review.

As indicated previously, many personality factors were found to be related to reactions to variations in the MBO process. For example, difficult goals were associated with increases in effort expenditures for managers high in self-assurance but with decreases in effort expenditures for managers low in self-assurance. Establishing priorities for goals was looked upon more favorably by managers lower in perceived intelligence and by managers higher in needs for structure. Our data indicate that it may be more important to allow subordinates who are high in self-assurance to participate in establishing goals than subordinates low in self-assurance.

The motives of the superior and subordinate can be also expected to be an important factor in reactions to the MBO approach. Our interview data indicated to us that there was a much more favorable reaction to the MBO approach among those managers who see MBO as a means of helping them achieve their personal objectives. Such personal objectives included a desire to force higher levels to communicate plans to lower-level personnel, a wish to be evaluated more objectively on the part of those with self-perceived deficiencies in personal characteristics or social backgrounds, a desire to force subordinates to coordinate their activities to a greater degree, and a wish for a means to prod certain subordinates to higher levels of performance. Our data from the questionnaire study indicated that there was a more favorable reaction to difficult goals from managers who believed that performance had a positive relationship to the reward system than among those managers who did not perceive much of a relationship between the level of performance and receiving pay increases and promotions.

JOB CHARACTERISTICS OF THE SUPERIOR AND THE SUBORDINATE. We found that the nature of the subordinate's job was related to the manner in which the MBO process was carried out. For example, as indicated in Chapter 2, some superiors simply draw up a list of goals and hand it to their subordinates; others have their subordinates draw up a list of job goals, which is then compared with a list of objectives established by the superior, and any differences between the lists are discussed and jointly worked out. Still others simply have their subordinates draw up a list of goals that may then be deleted in part or approved by the superior. Finally, there are some managers who accept a list of objectives from subordinates without discussion. We found that the subordinate's perception of the amount of his influence in the goal-setting process increases as we move from the former to the latter method of setting goals. Our research also indicates that the amount of participation in goal setting may be partially a function of the nature of the job being supervised. Where the subordinate clearly had to work on one particular objective, as in some engineering design activities, subordinate participation in the goal-setting process was limited. Where there were many different means or possible subgoals to a given end result, as in marketing activities, the subordinate's participation in the goal-setting process was higher.

ORGANIZATIONAL EXPERIENCES OF THE SUPERIOR AND THE SUBORDINATE. Another factor influencing reactions to MBO and the way that the MBO process is carried out is the past experiences of the superior and the subordinate. This could be an important determinant of initial reaction to MBO when such a program is first established. Many managers at Black & Decker did not initially have a positive reaction to the new MBO program and felt that it was simply another fad that would be soon forgotten, because they had experienced new programs in the past that were later abandoned. Our interview results suggested that this negative reaction based on past experiences may have significantly influenced the manner in which certain managers carried out the goal-setting and performance-review process. Past experiences with each other also influence the attitudes that superiors and subordinates have toward each other. The subordinate may trust his superior or be suspicious about what he says. For example, the subordinate himself may be positive toward a program endorsed by his superior if he has esteem for him. On the other hand, the subordinate may feel that his superior will not really care if he is unsuccessful in completing his goal assignments, because his superior failed to show concern in the past when assignments were not completed.

PARTICIPANT ATTITUDES

PERCEPTION OF BOSS AND ORGANIZATIONAL SUPPORT FOR MBO. Our research indicated that the MBO process was carried out more effectively when the individual manager believed that the organization fully supported the program and when he believed that his superior would be quite concerned with any goal failure on his part. By carrying out the MBO process more effectively, we mean establishing difficult and clear goals and then reviewing performance more frequently.

THE ATTITUDE OF THE SUPERIOR AND THE SUBORDINATE TOWARD MBO. Obviously, the more positive the attitudes toward the MBO approach, the more enthusiastically the program will be carried out by superiors and subordinates. We did find in our interview study that the attitudes of the head of an organizational unit are especially important, as one might expect, in determining how well an MBO program is carried out in that unit. We also found, in turn, that the attitudes of the head of an organizational unit and of many of his subordinates toward MBO are influenced by their perception of the usefulness of the MBO approach for the type of work that is done in that unit.

THE ATTITUDE OF THE SUPERIOR AND THE SUBORDINATE TOWARD EACH OTHER. We found that the amount of a subordinate's participation in the goal-setting process was significantly related to previous performance ratings of the subordinate made by the superior. The lower the ratings, the lower the amount of participation allowed. Thus, lower confidence in the ability of subordinates was associated with less participation. In another study, carried out with our data collected at two points in time, it was found that esteem for the boss increased when managers provided more feedback and support under an MBO program from one time period to another.[4]

MBO PROCESS STAGES

Our research has indicated that variations in the manner in which the goal-setting and performance review processes are carried out are related to variations in the results obtained in the MBO program. Most of these variations in results, however, seem to be influenced, in turn, by personality and situational differences among individual managers. Many such moderated relationships were reported earlier. There were a few relationships, however, that were consistent across all types of persons and situations. For example, establishing clear goals and providing frequent review of performance were related to all positive results and no negative results.

The MBO process variables are not necessarily related to each other. For example, our data indicate that the fact that a superior has a tendency to set difficult goals does not tell us anything about the frequency with which he carries out the review process. In addition, establishing goals in different ways may have a direct influence on results without the review process being necessarily influential at all. Some superiors do not even conduct an intermediate performance review. Sometimes, however, the two different components of the over-all MBO process are related. We found, for example, that as frequency of review increased, the clarity of the goals for the subordinates increased also.

The final performance review in the model precedes the results, because often some of the results are not fully known until after it has occurred. For example, the degree of goal achievement often becomes apparent only during the final review. Also, some of the later attitudinal reactions will depend upon how the superior responds to the level-of-goal achievement in the final review session. If he slights, for example, an obvious goal success by his manner, the subordinate may form a negative attitude about the MBO approach and his superior. The amount of praise and criticism given in the final review will have an especially important effect on the subordinate's attitudes, as the performance appraisal studies at General Electric demonstrate.[5] Researchers found that criticism from the boss created strong defensive behavior in the subordinate and that constructive responses to criticism rarely occurred. They also found that strong criticism so threatened self-esteem that it disrupted performance.

RESULTS

A number of possible results from an MBO program are listed in the model shown as Figure 7–1. Our data on these variables were collected at Black & Decker.

These results are judgments of success in achieving assigned goals, changes in attitudes and relations with the superior, attitudes toward the MBO approach, and changes in motivational levels. The results were often but not necessarily influenced by variations in the goal-setting and review process. For example, relations with one's boss could change even without the installation of an MBO program of any type. Or the subordinate may have considerable goal success regardless of how the MBO process is carried out, because the subordinate esteems the supervisor or because the subordinate is so engrossed and involved in his work that he will successfully complete his projects no matter what his superior does with MBO.

The model suggests that the results obtained may influence other factors. Successful or unsuccessful achievement of assigned goals will influence the superior's confidence in his subordinate as well as the subordinate's confidence in his ability to complete future goal assignments. Of course, goal failure by itself may not have a detrimental effect on the superior's or subordinate's attitudes toward the subordinate's abilities, as causes for lack of goal achievement may be entirely unrelated to the abilities of the subordinate in question. Goal success also influences to some degree a man's self-assurance and self-concept and to that extent does contribute to personality change, as the model shows. This contribution to personality change may be small or large, depending on the importance of the goal, its perceived difficulty to the subordinate, and his previously held self-concept and degree of self-assurance. For example, one more success is not likely to significantly increase the self-assurance of a manager already high in this factor.

If the MBO process is carried out in a positive manner by the superior, this will obviously have a positive influence on the subordinate's attitudes toward his superior and toward the MBO approach; the Black & Decker study did indicate that this was the case. Carrying out the MBO process may also improve the relations between superior and subordinate. They might as a result of this experience learn more about each other's characteristics, problems, and expectations—which may result in their learning to work together more effectively.

ADVANTAGES AND USES OF THE MBO APPROACH

As indicated in Chapter 1, MBO was initially seen, by many organizations, to be a more objective way of evaluating managerial performance. It also appeared to many to be a practical method of introducing participative management methods. Later, as organizations became more familiar with MBO, managers realized that MBO does aid in planning. But whereas these are certainly important uses of MBO, there are other important advantages to this approach as well. It is our contention that most managers do not utilize this approach to anywhere near its full potential, apparently because they have not thought deeply enough about what can be accomplished with it. Some of these other positive considerations are outlined here.

DIRECTS WORK ACTIVITY TOWARD ORGANIZATIONAL GOALS

We cannot assume that all activity in an organization is directed toward the attainment of organizational goals. However, an organization exists in order to achieve certain goals, and individuals are hired because they can make a contribution toward the attainment of those goals.

There are any number of reasons why work activity may not be congruent with organizational goals. Some members waste their time in performing tasks that are not very useful, simply because they lack the vision or the ability to see purposes. Others tend to see procedures as ends in themselves. There are numerous, often humorous, examples of procedures being carried out even though the "raison d'être" has long since passed. Perhaps it is not with tongue in cheek that Parkinson claims that two organizational members can keep each other quite busy passing unnecessary papers back and forth all their lives.

Some individuals see activities as desirable in themselves because of their fields of specialization. They identify with their fields and carry out activities because these are the things that people in the occupation do. An operations research man may carry out a particular type of study of very limited value, simply because this type of study is currently in vogue in the profession. A personnel manager may spend a great deal of time carefully interpreting a personality test of limited predictive validity in order to enhance his organization status or personal self-esteem. Some activities have a defensive purpose. The reaction of a line manager to a staff audit of his activities may be to assign some of his own men to audit these same activities so that he can defend himself, if the need arises. In addition, activities may be performed for the manager's own interests, as when the corporate sales manager suddenly feels the need to examine Florida operations in February.

The MBO approach does not necessarily preclude these problems. However, it does provide a powerful stimulus for the integration of work activity with organizational objectives, if carried out properly. Under MBO, managers must be able to relate their work activity to their specific performance objectives, which, in turn, are integrated with organizational goals.

FORCES AND AIDS IN PLANNING

Planning involves looking ahead to a desired end result and determining what must be done to obtain the objective. The objectives approach forces all managers in the organization to plan, which benefits the organization, the various organizational units, and the individual managers in the organization. This may, in fact, be the most important benefit from MBO.

Planning leads to better time utilization. Drucker points out the value of time as a resource both to a manager and to the organization:

> The supply of time is totally inelastic. No matter how high the demand the supply will not go up. There is no price for it and no marginal utility curve for it. Moreover, time is totally perishable and cannot be stored. Yesterday's time is gone forever and will never come back. Time is, therefore, always in exceedingly short supply.[6]

MBO forces managers to spend a significant amount of time on activities that will move the organization forward. Without such an emphasis on future goals, there may be a tendency to spend too much time on current problems.

Better planning should reduce the incidence of crash programs or emergency situations, which are usually the result of something's not having been done when it should have been. Such "fire fighting" invariably requires an inordinate amount of time and reallocation of resources to accomplish a goal that might have been reached more economically.

Better planning and clear objectives should lead to more rational work assignments. "Busy work" will be less because objectives and the plans to achieve them form the foundation for work assignments. Improved planning also means fewer problems, less tension, and a more pleasant work environment.

In addition, better planning may mean better utilization of scarce resources. Individuals, machines, or groups with special abilities but limited capacities can be allocated to the objectives that are most important or to which they can make the most significant contribution.

MBO should help integrate planning throughout the organization. Under this approach, objectives are first established at the highest level. Then departmental objectives and action plans pursuant to these organizational objectives are established. Thus the objectives at the top are factored into more specific and contributory objectives at lower levels. This process results in an integration and interrelationship of goals and plans throughout the organization.

PROVIDES CLEAR STANDARDS FOR CONTROL

Intelligent decisions are based on clearly formulated standards and/or goals. (In any organization many different types of goals or standards are possible, be they qualitative or quantitative). With MBO, the average manager will have clear-cut objectives that he can use to control activities and performances of his subordinates. Of course, objectives to be effective as controls must have certain attributes: They must, as noted, be clearly stated; they must be capable of measurement if only in a subjective way; they must not contradict other objectives; and they must be possible to attain. Other desirable characteristics of objectives have been discussed in Chapter 4.

As mentioned above

PROVIDES IMPROVED MOTIVATION AMONG MANAGERS

A number of fairly recent experimental research studies that we have cited indicate that the establishment of specific goals results in higher performance than when individuals are simply told to do their best. In organizations without the MBO approach, with the exception of occasional special assignments, personnel are simply expected to do their best. It is obvious, however, that specific goals mobilize and direct energy better than a general directive to do one's best. Thus, the specific goals associated with MBO can serve as incentives, even though they may not be attached to any specific material rewards. Research by Meyer and others at General Electric indicates also that among managers in an operating situation, performance improves most when specific goals are established for them.[7]

It has also been suggested that managers are more likely than any other occupational group to have high achievement needs.[8] According to Heckhausen, individuals with high achievement needs derive a sense of satisfaction from competing against some standard of excellence.[9] They are individuals who obtain personal satisfaction out of goal accomplishment for the sake of a sense of accomplishment alone. As Heckhausen notes, the standard of achievement may be task related, as when an individual is moving toward a perfection of performance, or may be self-related, as when an individual is trying to improve on earlier achievement. Obviously, the goals established under the MBO approach provide opportunities for attaining this sense of personal achievement. However, care must be taken in establishing goals for those with high achievement motives. Research indicates that high achievers wish to commit themselves only to goals that are neither too difficult nor too easy, because they consider the former type of goal a misuse of time and the latter type of goal as providing no sense of personal achievement when accomplished.

Several studies of motivation for managers and other organizational members provide strong support for the instrumentality theory.[10] This theory deals with the interrelationship of three factors: valence or strength of desire for a particular outcome; instrumentality, which, with respect to performance, refers to the individual's perception of the relationship between a certain level of performance and the achievement of a desired outcome; and expectancy, which refers to the individual's perception that a certain action by him will lead to a particular level of performance. For managers high in achievement needs, the desired outcome may consist only of a sense of achievement for its own sake. For managers low in achievement needs, it may be more important to clearly link performance to an outcome desired by the manager, such as a pay increase or promotion. Clearly, for these individuals, the MBO system must be tied to the organizational reward system in some way. It is clear also that the superior or higher-level management can influence the incentive value of an outcome. For example, the amount of a salary increase may be high or low. Instrumentality theory also indicates that in MBO the superior must be concerned with the subordinate's expectancy that he can, by certain efforts and action, attain the level of performance necessary to achieve a certain goal. The expectancy can be influenced by the level of performance goals established and by the amount of assistance and help provided by the superior.

A superior can also improve the motivational level among his subordinates by setting (or allowing to be set) individual goals that are in line with their interests or perceived abilities. In the first case, individuals will be more motivated for tasks they like doing. In making goal assignments among engineers, for example, their work preferences can be taken into account. In the second case, a goal can be assigned to an individual on the basis of the abilities required to meet the goal and on the basis of the abilities that the subordinate feels that he has. Several recent research studies indicate that individuals are more motivated for tasks that seem to them to require the abilities that they pride in themselves.[11] This is probably because, under these conditions, the successful attainment of the task validates their self-concept. On the other hand, if a person believes that he is a creative person and he fails on a task that he feels requires creativity, he may have to re-evaluate himself and perhaps change his self-concept. Our own research, discussed previously, on participants in a MBO program indicates the importance of the self-concept to performance. We found that managers with higher self-esteem responded to more difficult goals with higher-than-usual effort expenditures, whereas managers low in self-esteem reduced their effort expenditures when faced with difficult goals.

In general then, it would appear that, according to current research and theory on managerial motivation, the MBO approach can be an effective motivational tool if used correctly. However, before the proper objectives in terms of motivational force can be established for a subordinate, it will be necessary for the superior to know his subordinates well. He must have some awareness of each subordinate's personal goals, level of achievement needs, self-concept, including degree of self-esteem, interests, and expectancies concerning work assignments. This is obviously going to require time and effort and interest, as it is unlikely that one individual can know another well without some sincere interest in that individual as a unique person. In addition, it would seem from this discussion that a manager should be able to use the MBO approach more effectively for motivation after using it for some time, as this experience will provide him with valuable insight into the characteristics of his subordinates that we have indicated are important.

MAKES BETTER USE OF HUMAN RESOURCES

The idea that each man should do that for which he is best suited is not a new one. Plato in *The Republic* said that each man must practice that one thing for which his nature was best fitted.[12] Frederick Taylor argued the same point in his discussion of the "First Class" man.[13] In recent years, Rensis Likert has written extensively about the need for all organizations to utilize their human assets more effectively.[14] Although most organizations pay "lip-service" to this idea, they do not act in a way to make optimal use of the human resources that they employ. There is a considerable amount of evidence that a very significant proportion of organizational members possess skills, levels of knowledge, or mental potential that is not being used in their present positions.* Whenever this is the case, the organization's human resources are not being utilized to the fullest degree possible. This waste would be considered intolerable if financial or capital resources such as power or equipment were involved. Yet human resources are the only resources capable of extensive expansion in quality and thus are also being wasted when they are not developed and not allowed to grow and improve to the fullest extent possible.

The MBO approach can lead to a better utilization of human resources because, as pointed out in Chapter 6, objectives in many cases can be tailored to the unique abilities of a particular organizational member. In thinking about objectives for a particular individual, a manager can choose an objective that draws upon the unique ability in question. In addition, objectives can be established for organizational members in such a way that they provide a meaningful learning experience for the individual,

---

* See, for example, the range in abilities for individuals in different occupational groups in A. Anastasi, *Differential Psychology,* New York: Macmillan, 1961.

which, of course, contributes to his growth and development and increases the value of this particular human resource to the organization.

REDUCES ROLE CONFLICT AND AMBIGUITY

Role conflict results when an individual in a job is subjected to conflicting demands placed upon him by two or more people.[15] Role conflict has been found to result in lower job satisfaction, decreased confidence in the organization, and in higher levels of tension, which in turn are associated with psychosomatic illnesses of various types, such as ulcers and migraine headaches.

Role ambiguity is uncertainty about the way one's work is evaluated, about the scope of one's responsibilities, and about the performance-level expectations of others. Research conducted on role ambiguity indicates that it also results in lower job satisfaction, in a higher sense of futility, and in higher amounts of tension.[16] However, role ambiguity appears to have a greater impact on some personality types than on others.

Managers, like others, have security needs. These include the need to live in an environment that is relatively predictable and free from arbitrary and capricious forces beyond one's control. Our survey of managers found that among the items of information that managers wanted most from their superiors was information as to the standards of performance expected of them.[17] Uncertainty and ambiguity about a superior's wishes and expectations may produce certain dysfunctional behavioral consequences in the subordinate. He may spend inordinate amounts of time trying to find out from others what kind of a person his boss is and what his performance expectations are. He may waste time performing activities not actually related to any goals of his superior or organizational unit. If the insecurity becomes intense enough to result in fear and job anxiety, this may create a negative set toward the other aspects of the job.[18,19]

The objectives approach reduces uncertainty and ambiguity because it requires the superior to discuss with the subordinate his job goals and the standards of performance used to measure progress toward the attainment of these goals. During such discussions, problems in contradictory work expectations can come to light and can be eliminated or reduced in importance through problem-solving procedures.

PROVIDES MORE OBJECTIVE APPRAISAL CRITERIA

There are many limitations to the use of personality-trait ratings as an evaluation alternative.[20] Under the trait-oriented approach, the manager may be rated high on factors such as "cooperation," "leadership," or "originality." The problems with such dimensions are many. First, such characteristics are not easy to evaluate accurately, and this accuracy decreases as the traits become less closely related to performance. Second, to the extent that these personality traits are fixed and unchangeable, they evaluate what a person is rather than what he does. In addition, trait-oriented rating scales, to be of any value at all, require a considerable expenditure of resources to construct and to train raters in their use. Finally, trait-oriented ratings are probably less acceptable to both raters and ratees than ratings that are more performance oriented. A rater will not be motivated to use care in making his ratings nor will a ratee be motivated to change his behavior as a result of being rated, if ratings are not considered valid and worth while.[21]

Performance-oriented ratings tend to be more valid and probably are more acceptable to both rater and ratees; yet care must be taken. First, work activity by itself may not be meaningfully related to organizational goals. A manager may produce a very high level of work that is unrelated to any objective of the organization. In addition, under a performance-oriented system, there may be more of an emphasis on the means employed to reach a goal rather than on success in meeting the goal itself.

Under the objectives approach, recognition is given to the manager who gets things done rather than to the manager who makes a good impression or to the manager who conforms to his superior's expectations as to how something should be done. Performance reviews should also be less threatening under the objectives approach, as some of the mystery about what is expected is reduced. Defensive behavior is more likely to be induced with other appraisal methods, and although defense mechanisms do, of course, help the individual adapt to a complex and often hostile environment, extreme defensive reactions to personal criticism may generate long-term superior–subordinate hostility. This may give the evaluation discussion such an aura of apprehension, discomfort, and general unpleasantness that subordinates are unable to learn anything from them. Also, superiors may avoid evaluations entirely, or if required to carry them out, turn them into meaningless, ritualistic exercises.

Under the objectives approach, a manager and his boss should periodically discuss the progress attained toward goals. If the goals are not imposed on him but are developed with his participation, the manager is more likely to identify positively with them. In addition, less defensiveness may be generated under this approach if the discussions are not person centered. Maier reports research which indicates that problem-centered discussions elicit less defensiveness than person-centered discussions.[22]

All this is not to say that an objectives approach should be the only kind of appraisal system used. For the purposes of promotion and for purposes of rewarding professional development, other types of appraisal, such as group appraisal, may be used along with the goal-setting and review approach.

IDENTIFIES PROBLEMS BETTER

The frequent review sessions that should be part of the objectives approach should result in a better identification of problems. Problems by definition are barriers to goals.

Increased boss–subordinate interaction to discuss goal progress should help to identify problems early, before they get to be big. The presence of the experienced superior may result in the identification of problems of which the subordinate may not be aware. For example, a subordinate may report to his superior that even though another department is behind schedule in providing him with a service, he has been assured that they will catch up soon. However, if the superior knows from past experience that this department frequently fails to meet its deadlines, preventive action may be taken.

IMPROVES THE DEVELOPMENT OF PERSONNEL

The MBO approach can be very effective in increasing individual competence, if proper attention and emphasis is placed upon this as a goal of the MBO program. In Chapter 4 we recommended that self-improvement goals be established for each organizational member at the beginning of the year. These self-improvement goals should be based on an analysis of the reasons for any previous failure to accomplish goals. Any personal deficiencies identified by this process will be self-improvement goals in the next period. Self-improvement goals may also be designed to prepare one for a higher-level position. For guidance here an examination of typical goals assigned to individuals in this next-higher position can be used.

The use of MBO for developmental purposes allows more direct focus on those deficiencies of the subordinate that are relevant to performance in the organization. Yet often in training there is no attempt made to determine if the individuals assigned to a particular training course actually have a deficiency in the area covered by the course. Probably much management development is directed at overcoming deficiencies that may not be relevant to the particular organization conducting them.

Finally, the developmental efforts are individualized. They relate to the unique deficiencies of the individual rather than to those of a large group, which obviously makes the developmental efforts more effective. Miller in a study at General Electric concluded that if a person (who has the required abilities) is to improve performance he must[23]

1. Know what aspect of his performance is not up to par.
2. Know what corrective actions he must take to improve performance.
3. Have the ability to take the corrective actions.
4. Understand that his own interests compel him to take these actions.

Clearly, the process of identifying deficiencies and of establishing self-improvement goals for making them up does follow these steps, with the possible exception of step 3.

The development of organizational members is also facilitated by the MBO approach because, under MBO, coaching opportunities are improved. As Craig and Bittal point out, "There is general agreement among authorities that coaching is one of the most, if not the most, important ways by which to stimulate the development of managers. Managers are, in general, also agreeable with the authorities on the importance of coaching."[24] Yet getting managers to make the leap from theory and belief to actual coaching practice is difficult. The objectives approach facilitates coaching, as some of the reasons that make coaching difficult are eliminated. For instance, coaching is probably better accepted when it focuses on job-related factors. The review sessions in the objectives approach focus on job factors. Also, under MBO there is not just one performance review at the end of the year, as is the case with many conventional appraisal systems; there are many review sessions. In addition, under the MBO review sessions, as we indicated earlier, there is less defensiveness and therefore more acceptance of the superior's suggestions than under other appraisal systems.

MBO AS AN INTEGRATION OF TASK AND HUMAN ORIENTATION

The scientific management movement started by Taylor, Gantt, Emerson, the Gilbreths, and others was characterized by an emphasis on rational approaches for getting the work of the organization done.[25] In this school there was a focus on the task. Attention was directed at factoring the over-all objectives of the organization into smaller and smaller work assignments. The classical school of Fayol, Urwick, and others was concerned with planning, organizing work, and control but emphasized the upper levels of management more than the scientific management school did.[26]

The human relations movement, arising from the Hawthorne

Studies and conducted at Western Electric in the 1920's and early 1930's, changed the focus of attention from the task to the human being in the organization.[27] The movement stressed the study of the motivations and behavioral tendencies of organizational members as individuals and groups. Much attention was devoted to approaches for developing cooperative and task-achieving behavior and for facilitating the growth and development of personnel.

The task-versus-human-orientation conflict between the classical and human relations schools found its way into much of the early extensive research on leadership and supervisory behavior. In the Ohio State Leadership Studies, the two factors of "initiating structure" and "consideration" were identified as being of critical importance.[28] "Structure" refers to the leader's behavior in organizing his organizational unit with respect to authority relationships, communication channels, and work procedures; it involves a task orientation. "Consideration" involves leader behavior oriented to creating positive feelings such as warmth and trust between the leader and his subordinates. The research demonstrated that these two factors were fairly independent of each other. A leader could be high on the task orientation and low on the human orientation, vice versa, high on both, or low on both. Research on supervision, conducted at the University of Michigan, also described supervisors along two dimensions. These were "employee centered" or "production centered." Blake and Mouton, with their managerial grid, also characterized managers according to their concern for production and their concern for people.[29] The most effective manager according to Blake and Mouton is the 9,9 manager who shows simultaneously a high concern for production and a high concern for people. There is other research evidence that indicates that the combined emphasis on task and on the needs of the individuals who are to carry out the task results in higher productivity and higher employee satisfaction.[30] This also is consistent with Herzberg's theory, which points out that work itself can be the most important organizational factor in creating enduring satisfactions for organizational members.[31]

MBO, if used properly, can be an effective way to achieve simultaneously a task and a human orientation. Human needs for a recognition of individual uniqueness, for a feeling of accomplishment, for the utilization of abilities, for the growth and development of potentialities, for esteem from others, and for self-esteem may be met and realized in the MBO process. This is because the MBO process focuses on the individual and his unique abilities, interests, and personality characteristics. We have suggested previously that in MBO the superior should tailor the objectives, as far as possible, to the individual interests, abilities, and aptitudes of the subordinate. Our research findings point out the importance of providing frequent review of performance and proper help, support, and recognition to the subordinate during the review periods, no matter how short they are. In addition, MBO may be a powerful developmental tool and means of aiding in growth and development of all organizational members. It is important to ensure that the goals assigned to individuals not only maintain existing levels of organizational performance but are assignments that would move the organization to future higher levels of performance and perhaps new areas of activity. In addition, MBO can tie together all the plans of the organization.

Thus, MBO is an approach that can combine the task orientation of the scientific management and the classical school to the human orientation of the human relations school, and thus be a means by which any manager can more effectively carry out his supervisory responsibilities with both a "production-centered" and an "employee-centered" approach.

EXTENDING MBO TO THE RANK-AND-FILE LEVEL

MBO is an approach that is most often used for higher-level personnel. It is used primarily with managers and technical–professional personnel. We feel, however, that in some cases it is possible to extend the MBO process to lower-level personnel. Although higher-level personnel are somewhat different from lower-level personnel, who are relatively more concerned with security and social acceptance and less concerned with achievement, research cited in Chapter 1 indicates that rank-and-file employees respond positively to the establishment of specific goals.

The MBO approach would be easiest to apply to lower-level jobs involving the performance of a large number of unprogrammed tasks. If the work is less variable and the different tasks performed by the personnel are more programmed, it is probably better to use group instead of individual goals. The stronger affiliation tendencies of organizational members at the rank-and-file level may facilitate the achievement of group goals accepted by the group. The group goals can be in the nature of productivity goals, goals concerning quality or waste, or goals involving absenteeism and turnover. As in the case with the MBO process at the level of the individual, periodic performance review sessions should be conducted. In addition, the final review session should include an analysis of why any accepted goals were not achieved to the level desired.

This MBO process would involve the group members in the task, would reduce role ambiguity, and would provide for easier and better problem identification. The motivational force created by the specific goals would be increased by the motivational forces arising from group pressure. There is some research evidence that group goals developed with groups of blue-collar workers can increase productivity substantially. A series of studies conducted at Texas Instruments, where, after problem identification sessions, group goals were established with participation of the group itself, indicated considerable success for this approach.[32]

MBO IN THE FUTURE

It now appears that many middle-sized and smaller firms are adopting the MBO approach for the first time. It is not surprising that MBO is just being discovered by smaller firms, for, typically, any managerial innovation is accepted first by the largest firms, then in a few years by the middle-sized firms, and then after another few years by the smaller firms.

At the same time that smaller firms are discovering MBO, however, some older firms are going to have to take significant steps to improve their existing MBO programs, if atrophy is not to set in because of increasing disuse. In an earlier chapter we indicated that managers in the organization may resist full acceptance of the MBO approach because they view the program as involving too much paper work or too much of their time, or they see their subordinates as incompetent, or they see this approach as not applicable to their situation. We indicated also that MBO programs may not be properly integrated with other organizational systems, as in the English study by Wickens.[33] Lack of organizational support, lack of training, and failure of some key executives to carry out their program responsibilities are other causes of negative feelings about MBO. Of course, care must be taken to determine if any negative managerial reaction to an ongoing MBO program can be really attributed to deficiencies in the program. Stein, in an unpublished study, interviewed over 300 managers about their experiences with MBO.[34] He found that about half of those interviewed had some negative feelings about this approach. Upon analyzing their specific criticisms, he discovered that their complaints actually dealt with deficiencies in basic managerial ability, such as failure to keep subordinates informed of both the manager's and the organization's plans, and failure to delegate responsibility. Installing MBO will not turn poor managers into good ones. In this regard, our own research at Black & Decker seemed to indicate that the superiors who did the best job of setting goals and reviewing performance were managers who had the personality traits associated with general managerial effectiveness.[35] At any rate, many firms with MBO programs need to evaluate and reorganize them. They must identify the primary weaknesses of the program and take positive steps to eliminate these. It is hoped that many of the suggestions in this book will contribute to a revitalization of such programs. Many possibilities exist for handling the problems with MBO discussed here. For example, Stein has reduced the incidence of certain executives' failing to carry out their MBO responsibilities with the one-step review,[36] in which each manager must discuss the assigned goals of his subordinates with his superior.

Even firms with satisfactory MBO programs are probably not using the approach to its full potential. We have tried to point out in this book what this potential might be. However, as we have indicated, no MBO program can approach this potential without a considerable investment of support, time, and effort on the part of all the organization's managerial-level personnel. More specifically, we have indicated that a successful MBO program requires top-management commitment and support, training for organizational members in its use, clear and relatively stable goals communicated downward from higher levels, mandatory performance review, as well as information, reward, and budgetary systems that reinforce and are in harmony with the MBO program.

In the future we can expect MBO to continue to become part of standard managerial practice in middle- and smaller-level organizations. We would also expect that, with the current resurgence of interest in the topic, organizations with existing MBO programs will be increasingly interested in evaluating and improving their programs. In addition, we would expect extension of the MBO approach to the lowest levels in the organization and also into nonbusiness organizations, such as government agencies, hospitals, and educational institutions.

NOTES

1. Raia, A. P. "Goal Setting and Self Control," *Journal of Management Studies,* **2** (1965), 34–53, and "A Second Look at Goals and Controls," *California Management Review,* **8** (1966), 49–58.
2. Raia, 1965, op. cit.
3. Meyer, H. H., E. Kay, and J. R. P. French, Jr. "Split Roles in Performance Appraisal," *Harvard Business Review,* **43** (1965), 123–129.
4. Tosi, H. L., R. J. Chesser, and S. J. Carroll, Jr. "A Dynamic Model of Certain Aspects of the Superior/Subordinate Relationship," *Proceedings, Eastern Academy of Management, Annual Meetings,* Boston, Mass. 1972 (In Press).
5. Meyer, Kay, and French, 1965, op. cit.
6. Drucker, P. *The Effective Executive.* New York: Harper, 1966.
7. Meyer, Kay, and French, 1965, op. cit.
8. Atkinson, J. W., and N. T. Feather. (eds.) *A Theory of Achievement Motivation.* New York: Wiley, 1966.

9. Heckhausen, H. *The Anatomy of Achievement Motivation.* New York: Academic, 1967.
10. Porter, L. W., and E. E. Lawler III. *Managerial Attitudes and Performance.* Homewood, Ill.: Irwin, 1968.
11. Vroom, V. *Work and Motivation.* New York: Wiley, 1964. Korman, A. K. "A Consistency Model of Work Behavior," Symposium on Theoretical Developments in Industrial Psychology. *American Psychological Association, Annual Meetings,* San Francisco, Calif., 1968.
12. Plato, *The Republic.* Translated by B. Jowett. Oxford: Clarendon Press, 1888.
13. Taylor, F. W. *Scientific Management.* New York: Harper, 1947.
14. Likert, R. *The Human Organization.* New York: McGraw-Hill, 1967.
15. Kahn, R. L., D. M. Wolfe, R. P. Quinn, J. D. Snoek, and R. A. Rosenthal. *Organizational Stress: Studies in Role Conflict and Ambiguity.* New York: Wiley, 1964.
16. Kahn et al., 1964, op. cit.
17. Tosi, H. L., Jr., and S. J. Carroll, Jr. "Managerial Reaction to Management by Objectives," *Academy of Management Journal,* **11** (1968), 415–426.
18. Grove, B. A., and W. A. Kerr. "Specific Evidence on Origin of Halo Effect in Measurement of Morale," *Journal of Social Psychology,* **34** (1951), 165–170.
19. Paine, F. T., S. J. Carroll, Jr., and B. Leete. "A Study of Need Satisfactions in Managerial Level Personnel in a Government Agency," *Journal of Applied Psychology,* **50** (1966), 247–249.
20. Barrett, R. *Performance Rating.* Chicago: Science Research Associates, 1966.
21. Barrett, 1966, op. cit.
22. Maier, N. R. *The Appraisal Interview: Objectives, Methods, and Skills.* New York: Wiley, 1958.
23. Miller, L. *The Use of Knowledge of Results in Improving the Performance of Hourly Operators.* General Electric Company, Behavioral Research Service, 1965.
24. Craig, R. L., and L. R. Bittel. *Training and Developmental Handbook.* New York: McGraw-Hill, 1967.
25. Filipeti, G. *Industrial Management in Transition.* Homewood, Ill.: Irwin, 1946.
26. Filipeti, 1946, op. cit.
27. Filipeti, 1946, op. cit.
28. Korman, A. K. "Consideration, Initiating Structure and Organizational Criteria: A Review," *Personnel Psychology,* **19** (1966), 349–363.
29. Blake, R. R., and J. S. Mouton. *Building A Dynamic Corporation Through Grid Organization Development.* Reading, Mass.: Addison-Wesley, 1969.
30. Carroll, S. J., Jr. "Improving Employee Satisfaction and Productivity," *The Federal Accountant,* **17** (1968), 53–61.
31. Herzberg, F. *Work and the Nature of Man.* Cleveland: World Publishing, 1966.
32. Roche, W. J., and N. L. MacKinnon. "Motivating People with Meaningful Work," *Harvard Business Review,* **48** (1970), 97–110.
33. Wickens, J. D. "Management by Objectives: An Appraisal," *Journal of Management Studies,* **5** (1968), 365–379.
34. Stein, C. I., Personal communication, Carroll I. Stein and Associates, Minneapolis, Minn., July, 1970.

35. Carroll, S. J., Jr., D. Cintron, and H. L. Tosi, Jr. "Factors Related to How Superiors Establish Goals and Review Performance for Their Subordinates," *Proceedings, American Psychological Association,* 1971.
36. Stein, C. I., op. cit.

APPENDIX

A

INTERVIEW AND MAIL QUESTIONNAIRES

WPR STUDY—INTERVIEW FORM

Name of person interviewed _____

This interview is part of our study of the WPR program in this company. We are trying to find out how this program works and how it could be improved, if at all. Anything you say will be held in strictest confidence. The company will receive summary data only. The consultants conducting this study are doing it as a serious research study. The company is not paying anything for the study. In fact, the expenses of the study are primarily being met by the researchers themselves.

First I would like to ask you a few questions about the WPR process and its effects as it relates to one of your subordinates (a specific subordinate was named here).

1. Which of you had the most influence over the setting of the performance and self-improvement goals?
    Performance
    Self-improvement
2. What was the difficulty of the performance and self-improvement goals set?
    Performance
    Self-improvement
3. How much time was spent in establishing the goals during the goal-setting session and while preparing the session? Who spent this time?

	Him	Me
Before session		
During session		

4. How would you describe the climate when the goals were being set or discussed? (Warm and relaxed? Formal? Tense? Etc.)
5. How was the goal-setting session actually carried out? What happened first? Second? Next?
6. How did your subordinate respond in the goal-setting session? (What did he say? What did he do?)
7. To what extent did the performance and self-improvement goals focus on important things?
    Performance
    Self-improvement
8. Were there any later problems requiring a change in goals? Describe any such problems.

9. How much discussion was there about the goals and about the subordinate's performance with respect to these goals over the first year? (Amount of feedback, etc.)
10. How was this feedback carried out? (Informally? At scheduled conferences?)
11. What were the main difficulties, if any, in establishing goals for this man?
12. To what extent were the performance and self-improvement goals for this man met?
    Performance
    Self-improvement
13. In general, how would you rate the over-all performance of this man last year?
14. How does the attitude of this manager toward the job and the company this year compare with his attitudes last year?
15. How are your relations with this man this year as compared to last year?
16. How did the goal-setting session differ this year from last year, if at all?
17. Was the climate during the goal-setting session different this year from last year?
18. How do the performance and self-improvement goals set for this man this year differ from last year?

Now let's talk about the WPR program as applied to you and your job.

19. Which of you (boss or yourself) had more influence over the setting of the performance and self-improvement goals?
    Performance
    Self-improvement
20. How would you describe the climate when the goals were set? (Warm? Tense? Etc.)
21. How was the goal-setting session carried out? (What happened first? Second? Etc.)
22. How was the climate the second time around (this year)?
23. How did the goal-setting session differ this year from last year?
24. How do you feel about your job and company this year as compared to last year?

Now how about the program in general.

25. What are the purposes of the program as you see them? (What is the rationale for this approach?)

26. How, specifically, has the WPR program helped you?
27. How, specifically, has the WPR program hurt you?
28. Does the program give you a better understanding of your job? How?
29. Does the program give you a better understanding of your subordinates and your superior?
30. What are the effects of the WPR program on planning, if any?
31. What are the advantages of the program as you see them?
32. Do you have any suggestions for improving the program? What are they?
33. Are there any final comments you would like to make at this time about the program?

MAIL QUESTIONNAIRE

OVER-ALL PERFORMANCE APPRAISAL PROGRAM STUDY*

Please answer the following questions as truthfully as you can. The success of this study depends on your willingness to answer the questions in a truthful and careful manner. Your responses will be held in the strictest confidence by the two academic researchers conducting this study. The company will receive only summary data concerning the study.

In answering questions having to do with the Over-all Performance Appraisal Program, assume that the question is referring to fiscal 1969's goal-setting and appraisal effort unless the question specifically states that this is not the case.

1. What, in your opinion, was the level of difficulty of the performance goals set for your position?
   _____ Extremely difficult
   _____ Quite difficult
   _____ Moderately difficult
   _____ Not too difficult
   _____ Easy

2. What, in your opinion, was the level of difficulty of the self-improvement goals set for you?
   _____ Quite difficult
   _____ Moderately difficult
   _____ Not too difficult
   _____ Easy
   _____ No self-improvement goals were set

3. To what extent did the performance goals set for you under the program reflect the most serious and pressing needs of your department and the company?
   _____ To a very great degree
   _____ To a great degree
   _____ To a moderate degree
   _____ To a minor degree
   _____ Did not focus on any real needs of department or company

* This same program was previously called the WPR (Work Planning and Review) program.

4. To what degree did the self-improvement goals set for you reflect your personal development needs?

_____ To a very great degree

_____ To a great degree

_____ To a moderate degree

_____ To a minor degree

_____ Did not focus on real deficiencies

5. How often were you given feedback on your progress on your performance goals?

_____ Very frequently

_____ Frequently

_____ Occasionally

_____ Rarely

_____ Never

6. To what extent were your performance goals clearly stated with respect to results expected?

_____ To a very great degree

_____ To a great degree

_____ To a moderate degree

_____ To a minor degree

_____ Not at all clearly stated

7. To what extent was the relative importance of your various performance goals pointed out to you?

_____ To a very great degree

_____ To a great degree

_____ To a moderate degree

_____ To a minor degree

_____ No clues given as to the relative importance of performance goals

8. To what extent do you feel you control the means of reaching your performance goals?

_____ To a very great degree

_____ To a great degree

_____ To a moderate degree

_____ To a minor degree

_____ Do not control means of reaching goals

9. How often were you given feedback on your progress on your self-improvement goals?

_____ Very frequently

_____ Frequently

_____ Occasionally

_____ Rarely

_____ Never

10. To what extent do you feel you were given too many performance goals?

_____ To a very great degree

_____ To a great degree

_____ To a moderate degree

_____ To a minor degree

_____ Not given too many performance goals

11. How much emphasis did your boss put on attaining your self-improvement goals?

_____ A very strong emphasis

_____ A strong emphasis

_____ A moderate emphasis

_____ A minor emphasis

_____ No emphasis at all

12. How did the amount of effort you put into your job last year compare to that of previous years?

_____ Very much greater

_____ Much greater

_____ Somewhat greater

_____ About the same

_____ A little less

13. How do relations with your boss at the present time compare to your relations with him during previous years?

_____ Our relationship is much improved

_____ Our relationship is moderately improved

_____ No change

_____ Our relationship is somewhat worse

_____ Our relationship is much worse

14. How successful were you in attaining the performance goals set for you under the OPA program?

_____ Performance was much higher than the goals set

_____ Performance was a little higher than the goals set

_____ Performance was about equal to the goals set

_____ Performance was a little less than the goals set

_____ Performance was much less than the goals set

15. How successful were you in attaining the self-improvement goals set for you last year?

_____ Improvement was much higher than goals set

_____ Improvement was a little higher than the goals set

_____ Improvement was about equal to the goals set

_____ Improvement was a little less than the goals set

_____ Improvement was much less than the goals set

16. This year new performance goals have been set for you under the OPA program. How does the level of performance goals compare with the level of these goals last year?

_____ Very much higher

_____ Much higher

_____ A little higher

_____ About the same

_____ A little lower

_____ Much lower

17. This year new self-improvement goals have been set for you under the OPA program. How does the difficulty of these goals compare to those of last year?

_____ Much more difficult

_____ A little more difficult

_____ About the same

_____ A little less difficult

_____ Much less difficult

18. Who had the most influence on setting the performance goals for you?

_____ My boss had much more influence than I

_____ My boss had somewhat more influence than I

_____ My boss and I had about equal influence

_____ I had somewhat more influence than my boss

_____ I had much more influence than my boss

19. The amount of change associated with my job is
    _____ Much more than most other jobs at my level
    _____ More than most other jobs at my level
    _____ Equal to most other jobs at my level
    _____ Less than most other jobs at my level
    _____ Much less than most other jobs at my level

20. The number of contacts with persons outside my department are
    _____ Much more frequent than contacts with persons inside my department
    _____ More frequent than contacts with persons inside my department
    _____ Equal in frequency to the contacts with persons inside my department
    _____ Less frequent than contacts with persons inside my department
    _____ Much less frequent than contacts with persons inside my department

21. How much of an interest do you think the company has in the OPA program?
    _____ A great deal of interest
    _____ A moderate amount of interest
    _____ Some interest
    _____ Very little interest
    _____ No interest

22. How much of an interest do you think your boss has in the OPA program?
    _____ A great deal of interest
    _____ A moderate amount of interest
    _____ Some interest
    _____ Very little interest
    _____ No interest

23. Which statement best describes the manners in which your boss helps you in performing your job?
    _____ He rarely makes suggestions to me
    _____ He gives me some ideas, but I could use much more help

_____ Sometimes my boss helps me plan to reach a goal and sometimes he doesn't

_____ Generally, when I encounter a serious obstacle, my boss will suggest ways to overcome it

_____ Generally, when a serious obstacle arises, I discuss it with my boss and we revise the strategy *and* the goal

24. Which statement best describes the present difficulty your boss has in measuring your performance?

_____ My work is too complex to express in terms of standards of performance

_____ My boss is barely able to determine if I have done a a good job

_____ Sometimes my boss knows enough about the work I do to make judgments about my performance and sometimes he doesn't

_____ I have some measures of performance in practically every area of responsibility

_____ I have verifiable work goals: I mean, at the date agreed upon, my boss can tell readily how close I've come to accomplishing my goals

25. Which statement best describes the concern of your boss for your career?

_____ My boss feels this is my responsibility, not his

_____ He might discuss career plans with me but views this outside his responsibility

_____ He will discuss my long term career goals with me if I push him to do so

_____ We have agreed on specific things I need to do for my self-improvement

_____ My boss is interested in my development and views setting work goals as part of this process

26. Which statement best describes the kind of feedback you generally get from your boss about your performance?

_____ I'm lucky if I get any hint from higher management on how well I'm doing my job

_____ There are too many times when I really don't know what my boss expects of me

_____ The only real feedback I get about my performance comes through official channels

_____ I get some specific feedback about my performance, but I need more

_____ Much of the information I get about my performance is objective and not just subjective, and this helps

27. How often does your boss ask your opinion when a problem comes up that involves your work?

_____ Almost always

_____ Most of the time

_____ Sometimes

_____ Rarely

28. To what extent do you feel you can influence the decisions of your boss regarding things about which you are concerned?

_____ To a very great degree

_____ To a great degree

_____ To a moderate degree

_____ To a minor degree

_____ Not at all

29. In your opinion, how capable a manager is your boss?

_____ Extremely capable

_____ Quite capable

_____ Capable

_____ Not too capable

_____ Not capable

30. How good is your boss in dealing with people?

_____ Very effective

_____ Quite effective

_____ Moderately effective

_____ Not too effective

_____ Ineffective

31. All in all, how satisfied are you with your boss?

_____ Very satisfied

_____ Quite satisfied

_____ Fairly well satisfied

_____ A little dissatisfied

_____ Very dissatisfied

32. Considering your skills and the effort you put into the job, how satisfied are you with your pay?

_____ Very satisfied

_____ Quite satisfied

_____ Fairly well satisfied

_____ A little dissatisfied

_____ Very dissatisfied

33. If you had a chance to get a much better paying job working for another company in this area, how would you feel about changing?

_____ I would strongly prefer to stay here

_____ I would somewhat prefer to stay here

_____ I would have a hard time deciding

_____ I would somewhat prefer to change

_____ I would strongly prefer to change to the other compnay

34. In your opinion, to what extent will your actual job performance affect your future salary increases?

_____ To a very great degree

_____ To a great degree

_____ To a moderate degree

_____ To a minor degree

_____ It will not affect it at all

35. In your opinion, to what extent will your actual job performance affect your future promotions?

_____ To a very great degree

_____ To a great degree

_____ To a moderate degree

_____ To a minor degree

_____ It will not be related at all

36. In general, how much time did your boss devote to the OPA program?

_____ A great deal of time

_____ Quite a bit of time

_____ A moderate amount of time

_____ A small amount of time

_____ Very little time

37. Who had the most influence on setting self-improvement goals for you?

_____ My boss had much more influence than I

_____ My boss had somewhat more influence than I

_____ My boss and I had equal influence

_____ I had somewhat more influence than my boss

_____ I had much more influence than my boss

38. Did your boss indicate any priorities for your self-improvement goals?

_____ Yes

_____ No

39. How well do you like the OPA Program?

_____ I like it very much

_____ I like it pretty well

_____ I like it in some ways but not in others

_____ I don't like it very much

_____ I don't like it at all

40. In general, how applicable do you think the OPA program is to your job?

_____ Very applicable

_____ Quite applicable

_____ Fairly applicable

_____ Not too applicable

_____ Not at all applicable

41. How helpful has the OPA program been to you in performing the duties of your job?

_____ Very helpful

_____ Quite helpful

_____ Fairly helpful

_____ Not too helpful

_____ Not at all helpful

42. How interesting is the work in your present job?

_____ Extremely interesting

_____ Quite interesting

_____ Fairly interesting

_____ Neither interesting nor uninteresting

_____ Not at all interesting

43. Which of the statements best describes the amount of praise you received from your boss about your performance last year?
    _____ Received only praise with no criticism
    _____ Received mostly praise with just a little criticism
    _____ Received about an equal amount of praise and criticism
    _____ Received mostly criticism with just a little praise
    _____ Received only criticism with no praise

44. How concerned do you feel your boss would be if you failed to achieve the goals established for your job to a significant degree?
    _____ Very concerned
    _____ Quite concerned
    _____ Somewhat concerned
    _____ Just slightly concerned
    _____ Not at all concerned

45. What kind of criticism would you receive from your boss if you failed to achieve the goals established for your job to a significant degree?
    _____ Extremely severe criticism
    _____ Quite severe criticism
    _____ Somewhat severe criticism
    _____ Mild criticism
    _____ No criticism at all

46. How important is it for you to know what your boss wants you to do?
    _____ Extremely important
    _____ Quite important
    _____ Somewhat important
    _____ Slightly important
    _____ Not at all important

47. How important is it for you to have definite policies and procedures to help you in performing your job?
    _____ Extremely important
    _____ Quite important
    _____ Somewhat important
    _____ Slightly important
    _____ Not at all important

48. Did your boss establish priorities for your performance goals?

_____ Yes

_____ No

49. When your performance goals were established, what did you feel about the probability of their attainment?

_____ I felt I had more than a 90 per cent chance of attainment

_____ I felt I had about a 75 per cent chance of attainment

_____ I felt I had about a 50 per cent chance of attainment

_____ I felt I had about a 25 per cent chance of attainment

_____ I felt I had less than a 10 per cent chance of attainment

50. How satisfied are you with the present amount of influence you have on the decisions of your boss that relate to your work?

_____ Very satisfied

_____ Quite satisfied

_____ Fairly well satisfied

_____ A little dissatisfied

_____ Very dissatisfied

51. How important is it to you that you do a better job than other people who have or had your job?

_____ Extremely important

_____ Quite important

_____ Somewhat important

_____ Slightly important

_____ Not at all important

52. In your opinion, to what extent will effort increases on your part lead to increases in the level of your job performance?

_____ To a very great degree

_____ To a great degree

_____ To a moderate degree

_____ To a minor degree

_____ They will not be related at all

53. To what extent do you experience a feeling of personal accomplishment and satisfaction in fully completing your goal assignments?

_____ To a very great degree

_____ To a great degree

_____ To a moderate degree
_____ To a minor degree
_____ No feeling of personal accomplishment and satisfaction

54. Given your present situation in life, rank the following items in order of their importance, 1 through 7.
_____ Opportunity to use one's skills
_____ Opportunity to experience a sense of accomplishment
_____ Salary
_____ Recognition in current job
_____ Promotions
_____ Pleasant co-workers
_____ Job stability

*61. Are you working in a major new assignment?
Yes_____

62. Have you changed bosses within the last year?
Yes _____   No _____

63. Have you joined the company within the last year?
Yes _____   No _____

64. Did you participate in the Work Planning and Review Study done approximately one and one-half years ago?
Yes _____   No _____

Please make any other comments about the system that you feel are not adequately treated in the above questions.

* Questions 55–60 from original questionnaire omitted here.

It is of importance to the research being conducted that we be able to identify the respondents to this questionnaire. Under no circumstances will the identity of people responding to the questionnaire be made to the company, nor will any individual data be provided to any member of the firm. For this reason we are asking for personal identification. Please sign below.

_____

(Name)

SELF-DESCRIPTION INVENTORY*

Last name	First name

The purpose of this inventory is to obtain a picture of the traits that you believe you possess and to see how you describe yourself. There are no right or wrong answers, so try to describe yourself as accurately and honestly as you can. You are to blacken in the space between the two dotted lines (::::: ┅┅┅) for one word in each of the following pairs.

Be sure your marks are heavy and black.
Erase completely any answer you wish to change.

In each of the pairs of words below check the one you think *most* describes you.

1. ::::: capable
   ::::: discreet

2. ::::: understanding
   ::::: thorough

3. ::::: cooperative
   ::::: inventive

4. ::::: friendly
   ::::: cheerful

5. ::::: energetic
   ::::: ambitious

6. ::::: persevering
   ::::: independent

7. ::::: loyal
   ::::: dependable

8. ::::: determined
   ::::: courageous

9. ::::: industrious
   ::::: practical

10. ::::: planful
    ::::: resourceful

11. ::::: unaffected
    ::::: alert

12. ::::: sharp-witted
    ::::: deliberate

13. ::::: kind
    ::::: jolly

14. ::::: efficient
    ::::: clear-thinking

15. ::::: realistic
    ::::: tactful

16. ::::: enterprising
    ::::: intelligent

17. ::::: affectionate
    ::::: frank

18. ::::: progressive
    ::::: thrifty

19. ::::: sincere
    ::::: calm

20. ::::: thoughtful
    ::::: fair-minded

21. ::::: poised
    ::::: ingenious

22. ::::: sociable
    ::::: steady

23. ::::: appreciative
    ::::: good-natured

24. ::::: pleasant
    ::::: modest

25. ::::: responsible
    ::::: reliable

26. ::::: dignified
    ::::: civilized

27. ::::: imaginative
    ::::: self-controlled

28. ::::: conscientious
    ::::: quick

29. ::::: logical
    ::::: adaptable

30. ::::: sympathetic
    ::::: patient

31. ::::: stable
    ::::: foresighted

32. ::::: honest
    ::::: generous

* We deeply appreciate the permission given us by Professor Edwin E. Ghiselli of the University of California, Berkeley, to use this test developed by him.

In each of the pairs of words below check the one you think *least* describes you.

33. ::::: shy
    ::::: lazy

34. ::::: unambitious
    ::::: reckless

35. ::::: noisy
    ::::: arrogant

36. ::::: emotional
    ::::: headstrong

37. ::::: immature
    ::::: quarrelsome

38. ::::: unfriendly
    ::::: self-seeking

39. ::::: affected
    ::::: moody

40. ::::: stubborn
    ::::: cold

41. ::::: conceited
    ::::: infantile

42. ::::: shallow
    ::::: stingy

43. ::::: unstable
    ::::: frivolous

44. ::::: defensive
    ::::: touchy

45. ::::: tense
    ::::: irritable

46. ::::: dreamy
    ::::: dependent

47. ::::: changeable
    ::::: prudish

48. ::::: nervous
    ::::: intolerant

49. ::::: careless
    ::::: foolish

50. ::::: apathetic
    ::::: egotistical

51. ::::: despondent
    ::::: evasive

52. ::::: distractible
    ::::: complaining

53. ::::: weak
    ::::: selfish

54. ::::: rude
    ::::: self-centered

55. ::::: rattle-brained
    ::::: disorderly

56. ::::: fussy
    ::::: submissive

57. ::::: opinionated
    ::::: pessimistic

58. ::::: shiftless
    ::::: bitter

59. ::::: hard-hearted
    ::::: self-pitying

60. ::::: cynical
    ::::: aggressive

61. ::::: dissatisfied
    ::::: outspoken

62. ::::: undependable
    ::::: resentful

63. ::::: sly
    ::::: excitable

64. ::::: irresponsible
    ::::: impatient

APPENDIX

B

A SUMMARY OF THREE ARTICLES ON RESEARCH RESULTS FROM A QUESTIONNAIRE STUDY OF AN MBO PROGRAM

GOAL CHARACTERISTICS AND PERSONALITY FACTORS IN AN MBO PROGRAM*

RESULTS

Table B–1 presents the distribution of responses of 91 to 111 managers to each of the questions used in the criteria scales; the reader will note the great variability among the managers in their responses. Managers were

---

* This section is based on an article by the authors in *Administrative Science Quarterly*, **15** (1970), pp. 295–305. By permission of the publisher.

TABLE B–1   RESPONSES TO QUESTIONS USED IN CRITERIA SCALES

Question	Response Categories	*Per Cent Making Response*
1. How did the amount of effort you put into your job last year compare to that of previous years?	Very much greater	18
	Much greater	31
	Somewhat greater	47
	A little less	4
2. How do relations with your boss at the present time compare to your relations with him during previous years?	Our relationship is much improved	18
	Our relationship is moderately improved	14
	No change	65
	Our relationship is somewhat worse	2
	Our relationship is much worse	0
3. How successful were you in attaining the performance goals set for you last year?	Performance was much higher than the goals set	12
	Performance was a little higher than the goals set	17
	Performance was about equal to the goals set	47
	Performance was a little less than the goals set	18
	Performance was much less than the goals set	6
4. How successful were you in attaining the self-improvement goals set for you last year?	Improvement was much higher than the goals set	10
	Improvement was a little higher than the goals set	25
	Improvement was about equal to the goals set	45
	Improvement was a little less than the goals set	15
	Improvement was much less than the goals set	4

TABLE B-1—*continued*

Question	Response Categories	Per Cent Making Response
5. How well do you like the WPR program?	I like it very much	12
	I like it pretty well	21
	I like it in some ways but not in others	47
	I don't like it very much	10
	I don't like it at all	9
6. In general, how applicable do you think the WPR program is to your job?	Very applicable	13
	Quite applicable	22
	Fairly applicable	39
	Not too applicable	23
	Not at all applicable	3
7. How helpful has the WPR program been to you in performing the duties of your job?	Very helpful	11
	Quite helpful	8
	Fairly helpful	26
	Not too helpful	36
	Not at all helpful	19

evenly divided on their overall reactions to the program. In achieving goals, half of the responding managers equalled goals set, whereas the rest of the managers were evenly divided between those who failed to reach their goals and those who exceeded them. Half of the managers reported significant increases in expenditures of effort after the program was established, but only about one third reported improvements in relations with their superior.

CRITERIA VARIABLES. Of the four criteria variables, attitude toward WPR is most consistently related to differences in how goals were established. Managers had a more positive orientation toward the program when goals were relatively difficult ($r = .23$), clear ($r = .43$), and when a priority for self-improvement goals was established ($r = .30$). Subordinates reported improved relationships with their superior when goals were perceived to be clear and important ($r = .28$) and when goal priorities were set ($r = .18$), suggesting that the way in which goals are set may influence supervisory–subordinate relationships.

None of the goal characteristics was related to perceived increase in effort or to success in achieving established goals. Of course, goal achievement could be influenced by many factors external to the immediate work environment, and the differences in goal characteristics would no doubt be related to the varying perceptions of subordinates. The perceived amount of influence in setting goals was not related to any of the assumed output variables. This contradicts findings (Meyer, Kay, and French, 1965; French, Kay, and Meyer, 1966) that participation in setting goals was related to better relations with one's superior and with achieving goals. It also contradicts the frequent assertion that participation is a critical factor in the use and success of such a program (McGregor, 1957; Miller, 1968).

FEEDBACK AND REVIEW VARIABLES. Feedback frequency was related to goal clarity ($r = .54$), as one would expect. Also, goal clarity ($r = .23$) and goal difficulty ($r = .25$) were associated with anticipated sanctions, that is, a perception that the superior would be concerned with the subordinate's lack of success in achieving goals. Perhaps the establishment of clear and difficult goals is characteristic of bosses who have high performance expectations and who are therefore the type of superior who would be very concerned about any lack of goal accomplishment. Carroll (1968) found that superiors differed significantly with respect to their relative concern with high performance.

GOAL CHARACTERISTICS AND PERCEPTIONS OF HIGHER MANAGEMENT. Characteristics of goals were also related to differences in how higher management was perceived. Clarity of goals was associated with the perception that the superior spent more time on WPR ($r = .48$) and that there was more organizational support for the program ($r = .43$), and with greater satisfaction with the superior ($r = .34$). Priorities for self-improvement goals were associated with a perception that the superior was supportive ($r = .27$).

General participation was related to both goal clarity ($r = .25$) and subordinate influence on goals ($r = .21$). The general participation scale was an index of the level of influence that a manager feels that he has on the total job situation, and one might expect that as his participation in job-related decisions increased, his understanding of the job and its purposes would increase also. General participation had only a slight relationship to perceived amount of participation in the establishment of goals in the WPR program.

MODERATING VARIABLES. The relationships between goal characteristics and the output variables may be moderated by a third variable. Table B-2 presents the correlations between goal characteristics and the outputs as influenced by these moderating variables. Managers were classified into two groups on the moderating factor: high and low groups of about equal size. Correlations between the goal characteristics and the criteria variables were

TABLE B–2   THE EFFECTS OF MODERATING VARIABLES

Criteria Variables	Moderating Variable	Value of Moderating Variable	Correlations Between Goal-Setting Characteristics and Criteria Variables				
			Subordinate Influence	Difficulty	Clarity	Number	Priority
Increase in effort	Self-assurance	High	.33	.26*			
		Low	-.08	-.25*			
	Association of performance with reward	High		.26*			
		Low		-.19			
	Maturity	High		.31*	.39*		
		Low		-.26*	-.11		
	Decisiveness in decision making	High			.24*		
		Low			-.15*		
	Interest in job	High			-.02		
		Low			.32*		
	Support of superior	High			-.16	.26*	
		Low			.34*	-.13	
WPR orientation	Support of superior	High		.37*			
		Low		-.06			
	Intelligence	High					-.02
		Low					.58*
	Need for structure	High					.51*
		Low					.03*
Change in relations with superior	Decisiveness in decision making	High			.49*		
		Low			.09		
Goal success	Interest in job	High			-.12		
		Low			.32*		
	Association of performance with reward	High					-.04
		Low					.39*
	Decisiveness in decision making	High					.46*
		Low					.05

* Correlation is significantly different from zero at .95 level.

then made within each of these two groups. Only relationships where the difference between the correlations for the high and low groups was significant at the .05 level are presented in the table, that is, only relationships where the moderating factor seemed to make a difference in the relationships between goal characteristics and the assumed WPR variables.

Self-assurance. For managers scoring high on self-assurance, that is, believing themselves effective in dealing with problems, goal difficulty was positively related to perceived expenditure of effort ($r = .26$). Managers scoring low on self-assurance reported lower effort expenditures as goals became more difficult ($r = -.25$). Managers high on self-assurance may have believed they could attain difficult goals just by working harder, whereas managers low in self-confidence might have expected to fail to achieve difficult goals and thus expended less effort on their jobs than in previous years. Goal difficulty and effort were not correlated; only when self-assurance was considered, did a relationship emerge. This is a good example of the value of considering moderators in research of this type.

Individuals high in self-assurance also exerted more effort when they had influence over the goals set ($r = .33$). Influence over goals was not related to an increase in effort for those with low self-assurance. Self-assured persons should generally be more positively oriented toward themselves and those activities in which their ego is involved.

Maturity. Table B–2 shows that more difficult goals were related to perceived greater effort expenditures among the more mature ($r = .31$) and to lower effort expenditures among the less mature ($r = .26$). Perhaps the more mature managers, being more experienced, are better able to match the effort required to the difficulty of goals set; or, the more mature managers have greater confidence, and they can achieve difficult goals, whereas the less mature lack this confidence. More mature managers reported more effort with clear goals ($r = .39$). Perhaps this group is more likely to exert more effort when there is greater certainty about the goals that they are seeking.

Intelligence. Those with lower scores on self-perceived intelligence reported a more positive orientation toward the program if goal priorities were set ($r = .58$). When a superior established priorities in goals, the individual was no longer responsible for setting them; therefore, the risk that an error might be made in the selection of goals was lessened. The high-intelligence groups might be more aware of environmental cues and need less direction.

Decisiveness in Decision Making. Table B–2 indicates that managers who were more decisive decision makers reported higher levels of effort ($r = .24$) when goals were clear, and greater goal success when priorities for self-improvement goals were set ($r = .46$). Goal clarity was not related to increased effort by managers who were cautious decision makers, but it was related to perceived improvement in their relationships with their superior ($r = .49$). One might expect that the slow, cautious decision maker has a high regard for information and wants more certainty. Such a manager may be positively inclined toward a superior who provides this increased certainty.

Association of Performance with Rewards. Difficult goals were associated with higher perceived effort expenditures by those who believed that the reward structure, that is, pay increases and promotions, was closely related to performance ($r = .26$), but this relationship was not significant for those who did not believe that performance was tied to the reward system, as one would expect under current path–goal or instrumentality theory (Georgopoulas, Mahoney, and Jones, 1957; Vroom, 1964). Managers who did not link the performance and reward system reported that they were more successful in achieving goals when priorities were set for them ($r = .39$).

Interest in Job. For those with a low interest in their job, goal clarity was related to perceived increase in effort ($r = .32$) and goal success ($r = .32$). No such relationship appeared for those with a high interest in their job. Interesting work provides its own intrinsic motivation. Managers may work harder on jobs with high interest and involvement; but clear goals may have positive effects on performance for those in uninteresting jobs. Perhaps clear goals provide a challenge to the incumbent, giving him something to work for. An MBO program may make a dull job more challenging and improve performance. Bryan and Locke (1967) found that establishing goals increased interest on boring jobs.

Need for Structure. Managers with high needs for structure considered it important to know what their superiors wanted of them and to have definite policies and procedures to guide them in their work assignments. They seemed to have a more positive orientation toward the program when goal priorities were established ($r = .51$). Attitudes toward MBO on the part of those with a low need for structure were not related to the establishment of goal priorities. Thus, goal priorities, while desirable for most managers, might be especially important for those with a strong need for policy and direction.

Supportiveness of Superiors. Clarity of goals was positively related to perceived increase in effort ($r = .34$), with low levels of help and support from one's superior, but not significant for those who perceived their superior to be helpful and supportive. Perhaps managers with the supportive bosses were already exerting high levels of effort to please them. Other managers might need more information, perhaps interpreted as support, to increase effort. In addition, the number of goals was positively related to increase in effort ($r = .26$) for managers working for supportive bosses. Managers who esteemed their superiors because they were supportive could be expected to respond to more goals with the extra effort necessary to attain them. Also under high supportiveness was a positive relationship between goal difficulty and attitude toward the program ($r = .37$) but no relationship with low supportiveness. This might be the consequence of a perception by the subordinate that the establishment of difficult goals, especially self-improvement goals, is indicative of the supportive superior's concern for the development of the subordinate.

DISCUSSION

The results of the research on goal characteristics suggest that setting clear goals is positively related to many of the variables studied. The research also suggests that goal clarity may be more important to some managerial groups than to others. Clear goals were also related to higher levels of satisfaction with the superior and to a subordinate perception that the program was important. Our data indicate that goal clarity may be a function of other aspects of the MBO process. Objectives probably become clearer as the amount of time spent on the program by the superior increases, especially with an increase in the number of feedback and review sessions. Thus, in general, the results indicate that for all types of subordinates, the superior should make sure that the goals established focus on significant and important areas of departmental and personal need, that the goals are clearly stated, and that the relative importance of the various goals is pointed out.

The difficulty of goals, however, was not always related to positive reactions to the program. For example, difficult goals were related to decreased effort in managers with low self-assurance and among less mature and experienced managers. However, difficult goals were associated with increased effort among managers with high self-assurance, managers who associated their performance with the reward system, and mature managers. These findings indicate that it may be important for the superior to consider the characteristics of his individual subordinates before establishing the level of their regular performance and self-improvement goals.

A greater number of goals was not related to negative results. In fact, subordinates who worked for supportive superiors reported greater effort with an increased number of goals. There may have been greater acceptance of more work assignments when the superior was supportive; or, the subordinate may be willing to put forth more effort when he feels that he works for a supportive superior who will help him if he has difficulty.

Setting priorities for goals was related to a more positive feeling about the program and improved relations with one's superior for managers who perceived themselves as lower in intelligence, who were cautious in decision making, who associated higher performance with rewards, and who had a high need for structure.

Finally, the degree of subordinate influence in the goal-setting process did not seem to be an important factor in the perceived success of this program. Subordinate participation in setting goals did not result in higher levels of perceived goal success or effort nor in more favorable attitudes toward the program or the superior.

REFERENCES

Bryan, J. F., and E. A. Locke, **1967.** "Goal Setting as a Means of Increasing Motivation," *Journal of Applied Psychology,* **51:** 274–277.

Carroll, S. J., Jr., **1968.** "Improving Employee Satisfaction and Performance," *The Federal Accountant,* **17:** 53–61.

French, J. R. P., Jr., E. Kay, and H. H. Meyer, **1966.** "Participation and the Appraisal System,' *Human Relations,* **19:** 3–19.

Georgopoulas, B. S., G. M. Mahoney, and M. N. W. Jones, **1957.** "A Path-Goal Approach to Productivity," *Journal of Applied Psychology,* **41:** 345–353.

McGregor, D., **1957.** "An Uneasy Look at Performance Appraisal," *Harvard Business Review,* **35:** 89–94.

Meyer, H. H., E. Kay, and J. R. P. French, **1965.** "Split Roles in Performance Appraisal," *Harvard Business Review,* **43:** 123–129.

Miller, E., **1968.** *Objectives and Standards of Performance in Financial Management. Study* 87. New York: American Management Association.

Vroom, V., **1964.** *Work and Motivation.* New York: Wiley.

THE RELATIONSHIP OF CHARACTERISTICS OF THE REVIEW PROCESS AS MODERATED BY PERSONALITY AND SITUATIONAL FACTORS TO THE SUCCESS OF THE MBO APPROACH*

RESULTS

Table B–3 presents the correlations between the three review-process characteristics and the criteria, goal characteristics, and supervisory variables. Only correlations that were significant at the .05 level are shown.

* This section is based on an article by the authors in *Proceedings, Academy of Management,* 1939, 134–143. By permission of the publisher.

TABLE B–3   RELATIONSHIP BETWEEN REVIEW-PROCESS
CHARACTERISTICS AND MBO CRITERIA,
GOAL, AND SUPERVISORY VARIABLES*

	Review-Process Characteristics		
	Frequency of Feedback	*Amount of Positive Feedback*	*Anticipated Sanctions for Goal Failure*
Criteria variables			
Effort increase			
MBO orientation	.50		.20
Goal success	.17	.25	
Change in superior relations	.33		
Goal characteristics			
Clarity of goals	.54		.25
Difficulty of goals			.23
Superior's characteristics			
Superior's time on MBO	.64	.19	.33
Organizational support for MBO	.57		.29
Subordinate influence allowed	.24		
Esteem and satisfaction for supervisor	.52		.30
Help and support from superior	.34		.29

* Only relationships significant at the .05 level are shown.

REVIEW-PROCESS CHARACTERISTICS AND CRITERIA VARIABLES. As shown in Table B–3, the frequency of feedback is quite strongly related to positive feelings about the MBO program ($r = .50$), is related moderately well to an improvement in relations with one's boss ($r = .33$), and is slightly related to success in achieving goals ($r = .17$). These findings are not unexpected and may indicate that the frequency of performance review is a critical factor in MBO program success. The table also shows that the amount of positive feedback is related to success in achieving goals ($r = .25$) and that there is a significant relationship between amount of threat or superior concern for goal failure and a positive opinion toward the program ($r = .20$). One would expect a communication by the superior of concern for goal failure would also communicate to the subordinate that the MBO program was important.

GOAL CHARACTERISTICS. Table B–3 also indicates that frequency of feedback is quite highly related to goal clarity ($r = .54$). This might indicate that a number of review sessions are needed before a subordinate really understands the goals that he is expected to accomplish. In addition, the table shows that clear and difficult goals are related to a perception by the subordinate that the boss will be very concerned about goal failure ($r = .25$ and $r = .23$). The establishment of clear and difficult goals in itself could communicate to the subordinate that his boss is concerned with success in implementing the MBO approach.

SUPERVISORY CHARACTERISTICS. Table B–3 shows that differences in the manner in which the review process is carried out are significantly related to differences in managers' perceptions of their superiors. This is especially true of the frequency of feedback, which is positively related to managerial perceptions that higher management is supporting the MBO program ($r = .57$), that the superior is spending more time in the MBO program ($r = .64$), and that the subordinate does have influence with his boss and that his boss does allow him to participate on problems that affect him ($r -.24$). Feedback is also positively related to esteem and satisfaction with the superior ($r = .52$) and to a feeling that the superior is concerned about the subordinate and interested in his well-being ($r = .34$).

In addition, the table indicates that there is a slight relationship between the amount of praise (rather than criticism) received and the subordinate's perception that his boss spent more time on the WPR program ($r = .19$). Also, anticipated sanction for goal failure (threat) is related to a number of supervisory and organizational variables. For example, the table shows that there is a positive relationship between perceptions that the superior will be concerned with goal failure and the amount of time that the superior spends on the MBO program as reported by his subordinate ($r = .33$). Perhaps by spending a lot of time on the MBO program, the superior communicates in this way to the subordinate that the MBO program is important and that it is important to achieve goals assigned to the manager under the program. Table B–3 also shows a significant relationship between perceptions that the superior is helpful and supportive and perceptions that the superior will be concerned and critical if goals are not achieved ($r = .29$). This might indicate that subordinates associate a superior's helpful and supportive behavior as being indicative of his concern for the subordinate and what he accomplishes. Also, a perception of higher management support for the MBO program is significantly related to subordinate perceptions that his superior will be concerned if the subordinate does not achieve his goals ($r = .29$). Finally, the table indicates that anticipated superior concern for goal failure is significantly related to higher rather than lower satisfaction with the superior $(r = .30)$. This also is not surprising: organizational members are more positive about those who are concerned about them.

MODERATED RELATIONSHIPS BETWEEN REVIEW-PROCESS CHARACTERISTICS AND CRITERIA VARIABLES. As indicated previously, it was hypothesized that the relationship between variations in the way the review process was carried out and various assumed consequences of these variations would be influenced by certain personal and situational characteristics. Therefore, a certain number of job, personality, and supervisory relationship variables were held constant while the review-process variables were related to the criteria variables. Table B–4 presents these moderated correlation coefficients. In obtaining these, managers were divided into two approximately equal groups on each moderating factor, and then correlations were made within each group. Many significant correlations were obtained in this analysis, but only these relationships in which the *difference* between the correlations for the high and low moderated groups was significant at the .05 level are presented in the table. In other words, the table only presents relationships between review-process characteristics and criteria variables where the moderator seemed to make a significant difference. Thus, for the moderators not shown in the table, the correlations between the review-process characteristics and the criteria variables were similar for the high and low groups.

PERSONALITY CHARACTERISTICS. Table B–4 indicates that several personality characteristics as measured by the Ghiselli Self-Description Inventory seem to moderate the relationship between review-process characteristics and certain assumed consequences of variations in such characteristics.

Self-assurance. Managers high on self-assurance perceive themselves as being effective in dealing with problems that face them. Table B–4 indicates that the frequency of feedback is moderately related to goal success for those low in self-assurance $(r = .38)$ but not for those high in self-assurance. In Table B–3, for the group managers as a whole, feedback frequency was only slightly related to goal success $(r = .17)$. Thus, the self-assurance of the manager seemed to make a difference here. Managers who are high on self-assurance could be expected to have been more effective and successful in the past and would therefore probably have the ability to accomplish goals by their own efforts. Managers low on the self-assurance scale may have been less successful in the past and thus need more information about their level performance in order to prevent discouragement and loss of motivation.

The table also indicates that higher amounts of criticism are associated significantly with higher effort expenditures by those managers low in self-assurance $(r = -.24)$ but not for those high in self-assurance. This finding

TABLE B–4   RELATIONSHIP BETWEEN REVIEW-PROCESS CHARACTERISTICS
AND MBO CRITERIA VARIABLES AS MODERATED BY
PERSONALITY, SUPERVISORY, AND JOB FACTORS*

	Review-Process Characteristics					
	Frequency of Feedback		Amount of Positive Feedback		Anticipated Sanctions for Goal Failure	
	High	Low	High	Low	High	Low
Personality characteristics						
Self-assurance						
Effort increase			+.11	−.24**		
Goal success	−.02	.38**				
Decision-making approach						
Effort increase	+21	−.29				
Goal success					−.21	+26**
Supervisory characteristics						
Help and support from superior						
Effort increase	+27**	−.20				
Subordinate influence allowed						
MBO orientation					+.32	−.07**
Superior priorities for goals						
Goal success	+.35**	−.05				
Job characteristics						
Job satisfaction						
Effort increase					+.09	−.32**
Association of performance with reward system						
Effort increase			−.33**	.09		
Frequency of job change						
Effort increase change in superior relations	.58**	.05			−.32**	.18

* Pairs of correlations shown only where difference between coefficients is significant at the .05 level.
** At least .05 level of significance.

might indicate that those low in self-assurance are more receptive to criticism than those high in self-assurance, and act upon it.

Decision-Making Approach. Among managers who are cautious decision makers, higher amounts of effort are associated with lower frequencies of feedback ($r = -.29$). Perhaps with lower levels of feedback, goals are less clear and the cautious manager increases his efforts to ensure that he does achieve his goals. The table also indicates that among the more cautious managers there is a significant positive relationship between success in achieving goals and the amount of concern and criticism that they feel would come from their superior if goals were not met ($r = .26$).

SUPERVISORY VARIABLES. A number of aspects of the superior–subordinate relationship also appeared to moderate the relationship between review-process characteristics and the criteria variables used in the study.

Help and Support from Superior. Table B–4 indicates that among managers who perceive their boss as providing high degrees of support and help to them, there is a positive relationship between feedback frequency and effort expenditures ($r = .27$). Among managers who perceive their superiors as not providing much support and help to them, there is a tendency, although it only approaches statistical significance, for higher frequency of review to be associated with lower effort expenditures ($r = -.20$). These results are not unexpected. You would expect that subordinates would respond to higher pressure with higher effort if they felt their superiors would back them and help them. On the other hand, higher pressures in the form of more performance reviews might be considered quite unfair by subordinates if they are coupled with little help and assistance from the superiors in achieving goals.

Subordinate Influence. Table B–4 shows that among managers who are allowed more participation by their superiors in decisions on matters that affect them, there is a positive relationship between a perception that the boss would be concerned about goal failure and their attitude toward the MBO program ($r = .32$). This was not true of managers who were typically allowed only slight participation by their superiors. The correlation between boss concern about goal failure and MBO orientation was $r = .20$, when the degree of typical job influence was not taken into account. The relationship may be simply the result of some type of reciprocity relationship. Superiors who allow their subordinates to participate in decisions that affect them have subordinates who appreciate this (subordinate influence correlates $r = .38$ with satisfaction with superior) and are more positive about programs that the superior considers important.

Boss Priorities. One question asked if the boss established priorities for self-improvement goals. When priorities were established for goals, feedback frequency did have a significant positive relationship to goal success ($r = .35$). Where no priorities were indicated for these goals, there was no significant relationship between feedback frequency and goal success. Table B–3 shows a relationship between frequency of feedback and goal success of only $r = .17$. Thus it would appear that both frequent feedback and clear goals together contribute to goal success to a greater degree than one of these factors alone.

JOB CHARACTERISTICS. A number of job characteristics also seemed to influence the relationship of review-process characteristics to criteria variables.

Association of Performance with Reward System. Table B–4 shows that among managers who associated improved performance with the receiving of organizational rewards, higher amounts of criticism were associated with higher effort expenditures $(r = -.33)$. There was no relationship between the amount of praise or criticism and effort increase for those managers not associating performance with the reward system. This finding is, of course, very much in line with current instrumentality theory findings, which indicate that effort expenditures and performance are higher when managers see a relationship between performance and the reward system. We, of course, should not be surprised to see a significant relationship between criticism and effort but not between criticism and goal success, because, unlike effort, goal success depends on factors outside the manager's control.

Job Satisfaction. Job satisfaction measures the satisfaction with pay and the degree of the subordinate's reluctance for changing jobs. For those with less job satisfaction there is a negative relationship between effort increase and perceptions that the superior will be concerned about lack of goal accomplishment $(r = -.32)$. Hence the superior's concern for failure to achieve goals and perhaps also higher pressure may reinforce an already negative situation, leading to generally lower levels of effort to get the job done.

Frequency of Job Change. This variable measures the stability of job requirements. Some jobs have quite consistent requirements from one period to another, whereas the activities of other jobs change frequently. Table B–4 indicates that among those managers with jobs with requirements that change rapidly, frequency of feedback is positively related to better relations with the boss $(r = .58)$; that is, relations with the boss are better when there is more feedback and worse when there is less. This is not unexpected, especially on jobs characterized by rapidly changing demands. Changing demands may be frustrating to those people involved in them if they are not fully informed and do not receive some feedback about their performance. In addition, among such high-changing jobs there is a significant negative relationship between effort increase and perceived sanctions for lack of goal accomplishment $(r = -.32)$. This could be the result of such managers' feeling that it is unfair for superiors to expect them to accomplish planned goals when the plans are constantly changing.

SUMMARY AND DISCUSSION

The results show that differences in the way that the review process under the MBO approach is carried out are associated with what may be assumed to be positive and negative outcomes of an MBO program. The results also indicate that the relationship between such differences in characteristics of the review process and some criteria of MBO success vary for different types of managers and situations.

More specifically, the results show that higher frequencies of review are associated with higher values on variables that would be considered to be beneficial in terms of various indices or organizational short- and long-range effectiveness. For example, higher feedback frequency of review was related to more favorable attitudes toward the MBO program ($r = .50$), higher goal success ($r = .17$), improvement in relationships with the boss ($r = .33$), clarity of goals ($r = .54$), a feeling that the subordinate has influence in matters affecting him ($r = .24$), and esteem and satisfaction for the superior ($r = .52$). When moderated by personality and situational factors, there were stronger relationships with the various output variables and feedback frequency. For example, among those managers low in self-assurance, feedback frequency correlated with goal success ($r = .38$), and when associated with the establishment of priorities for goals, feedback frequency correlates $r = .35$ with goal success.

Higher amounts of praise and lower amounts of criticism are associated with higher goal success, but it is impossible to say in this situation what is the cause of the other. In other significant relationships previously discussed, one can make certain inferences on the basis of the relationship that seem more logical than alternative inferences, but here one inference is as good as the other. The relative amount of praise or criticism given to subordinate managers in the review process was associated with effort increases for different types of managers. Higher amounts of criticism and lower amounts of praise were associated with greater effort expenditures among managers low in self-assurance and among managers who believed that organizational rewards were related to performance. These, of course, are the managers whom we would expect to be motivated to increase their effort in response to criticism of their progress toward the attainment of goals.

The amount of perceived superior concern and criticism for a subordinate's goal failure is associated with feelings that the superior is concerned and involved with the MBO program and with a good relationship between the superior and subordinate. It is also associated with the establishment of clear and difficult goals. These findings support the assumption that a superior shows his concern about the subordinate's performance under MBO by the way he carries out the MBO process and by the way he relates to his subordinates. One might also hypothesize from the findings that showing higher concern about a subordinate's performance may not always be beneficial in terms of results obtained. For two groups of managers there were lower levels of effort when high concern of the superior for goal performance was perceived to be present.

SOME FACTORS AFFECTING THE SUCCESS OF MBO*

RESULTS

Table B–5 presents the correlations between the five managerial variables and the criteria. The results suggest that an important factor is the perceived amount of time that the boss spends on MBO. For instance, it is related to higher levels of satisfaction with MBO ($r = .50$), perceived goal success ($r = .20$), and improved boss relations ($r = .26$). It is negatively related to perceived effort increases ($r = -.23$).

  Top-management support is the consultant's *sine qua non* for success of any program. This factor is correlated with only one criterion variable, the orientation to WPR ($r = .49$). The magnitude of this relationship suggests the significance of "support" for subordinate satisfaction with an MBO program. But support alone is not related to other general effects.

TABLE B–5 CORRELATIONS BETWEEN SUPERVISORY VARIABLES AND WPR OUTPUT VARIABLES

WPR Output Variables	Time Spent in WPR	Organizational Support	Psychological Participation	Satisfaction with Boss	Boss Involvement
WPR orientation	.50***	.49***		.23**	
Effort increase	−.23**				
Goal success	.20**			.18*	
Change in boss relations	.26***		.26***	.29***	.17*

  * $P > .10$.
  ** $P > .05$.
  *** $P > .01$.

* This section is based on an article by the authors in *Journal of Management Studies* 7 (1970), 209–223. By permission of the publisher.

Some proponents of the objectives approach argue that many of its advantages result from increased subordinate participation. In another study, a specific measure of subordinate influence on job goals was not related to any of the criterion variables.[1] Here, a more general measure of influence, which Vroom[2] called psychological participation, was found to be related only to changes in relationship with the boss $(r = .26)$. It does not seem that the *general* effect of participation is substantial enough to argue it with the intensity that some have. Rather, it was found that the participation has differential effects on a function of some of the moderator variables.

Satisfaction with the boss is positively related to satisfaction with MBO $(r = .26)$, goal success $(r = .18)$, and to improved boss relationships $(r = .29)$. Superior involvement in the job was only slightly related to an improved relationship with the boss $(r = .17)$.

RELATIONSHIP BETWEEN MANAGERIAL FACTORS AND OTHER PROCESS VARIABLES. It is to be expected that there is some interaction between the three groups of process variables. The relationship among the managerial factors, goal characteristics, and the feedback and review variables will be briefly discussed.

Feedback and Managerial Factors. Table B–6 presents the correlations between these two sets of process variables. All the managerial variables are related to the perceived frequency of feedback. Frequent feedback is positively related to the perceived time that the boss spends on MBO $(r = .65)$, the perceived level of support for MBO $(r = .55)$, psychological participation $(r = .27)$, satisfaction with the boss $(r = .53)$, and boss involvement $(r = .34)$.

TABLE B–6   CORRELATIONS BETWEEN SUPERVISORY VARIABLES AND FEEDBACK CHARACTERISTICS

Feedback Variables	Time Spent in WPR	Organizational Support	Psychological Participation	Satisfaction with Boss	Boss Involvement
Feedback frequency	.65***	.55***	.27***	.53***	.34***
Amount of positive feedback	.26**				
Anticipated sanctions	.35***	.28***		.33***	

*** $P > .01$.

* This section is based on an article by the authors in *Journal of Management Studies* **7**, (1970), 209–223. By permission of the publisher.

The anticipated sanctions measure was related to a number of the managerial variables. Higher perceived levels of the boss's willingness to implement sanctions were related to the boss's time on MBO ($r = (.35)$, organizational support ($r = .28$), and satisfaction with the boss ($r = .33$).

The amount of positive feedback was related only to the perceived time that the boss spent on MBO ($r = .26$).

These results suggest that the subordinate's view of the superior's behavior is related to the subordinate's perception of feedback frequency and the willingness of the boss to use sanctions if goals are not met. The boss is viewed more positively when feedback is frequent. Perhaps feedback and the willingness to use sanctions may be interpreted as the degree of boss and organizational commitment. Perhaps feedback from the boss increases the salience of the program for the organization member.

Goal Characteristics and Supervisory Variables. Goal clarity is related to a number of supervisory variables (see Table B–7). Those who

TABLE B–7 CORRELATIONS BETWEEN SUPERVISORY AND GOAL CHARACTERISTIC VARIABLES

Goal-Setting Process Variables	Time Spent in WPR	Organizational Support	Psychological Participation	Satisfaction with Boss
Goal clarity	.49***	.40***	.26***	.35***

*** $P > .01$.

report clearer goals also feel that their superior spends more time on WPR ($r = .49$) and perceive a greater degree of organizational support for WPR ($r = .40$). The clearer the goals, the more satisfied the individual is with his boss ($r = .36$). Goal clarity is also related to the perceived level of subordinate's psychological participation ($r = .26$) in the total job situation. Perhaps when the subordinate can, or believes he can, help shape the goals, he feels more able to understand them.

Goal clarity is related to positive attitudes toward the boss. It may be that the subordinate responds to clearer goals in a more positive fashion. Superiors who set them are simply perceived more positively. The obverse may also be the case. If there is positive effect toward another, greater clarity of his expectation is perceived than might objectively be the case.

MODERATED RELATIONSHIPS BETWEEN THE MANAGERIAL FACTORS AND THE CRITERIA. The moderators, described earlier, were used to examine the effects of the dependent and independent variables under different conditions. The analysis resulted in the relationships that follow (see Table B–8).

TABLE B–8 CORRELATIONS BETWEEN SUPERVISORY VARIABLES AND WPR OUTPUT VARIABLES AS MODERATED BY PERSONALITY, JOB, AND ORGANIZATIONAL FACTORS

	Time Spent in WPR		Organizational Support		Psychological Participation		Satisfaction with Boss		Boss Involvement	
	High	Low	High	Low	High	Low	High	Low	High	Low
Need for policy										
Goal success					.48***	-.02			-.38***	.09
Change in boss relations										
Initiative										
WPR orientation					.24*	-.17			.32**	-.13
Control over means										
Goal success									.11	-.22*
Change in goal level							.37***	-.04*		
Change in boss relations					.00	.41***				
Satisfaction with the situation										
Effort increase							.09	-.39***		
Goal success									-.27**	.17
Change in boss relations									-.05	.33***
Job interest										
Effort success	-.43***	.20	-.26**	.18			-.29**	.08		
Goal success					-.05	.29*				
Change in boss relations									.29**	-.21*
Frequency of job change										
Effort increase			.03	-.31**						
Goal success	.45***	-.10							.13	-.23*
Change in boss relations										
Goal priorities										
Effort increase					.21*	-.32***	.19	-.40***		
Goal success	.47***	-.04	.21*	-.17	.46***	-.14	.39***	.04	.10	-.30**

* p ⩾ .10. ** p ⩾ .05. *** o > .01.

Need for Policy. Individuals with a high need for policy report higher levels of boss involvement related to lower levels of perceived goal success ($r = -.38$). However, for these same managers with high policy needs, participation (or general job influence) was related to better boss relationships ($r = .48$). It may be that these managers react negatively to what appears to be one-way involvement, whereas the obtaining of job parameters through general interaction may be more positively valued.

Initiative. Psychological participation is related to the subordinate's orientation to MBO for high-initiative managers ($r = .24$) and negatively related ($r = .17$) for low-initiative respondents. Those with high initiative may want to be more involved and know what is going on. If they participate, they are more positive in their reaction to programs of higher management. On the other hand, those with low initiative may be more passive, have a less active role in the organization, resulting in more negative attitudes toward management programs in which involvement is forced.

In addition, high-initiative managers also report more satisfaction with MBO with higher levels of boss involvement ($r = .32$). There was no significant relationship between these two variables for the low-initiative group. Perhaps high-initiative managers want assistance, support, and help from their boss in their jobs and careers. When this help and support is forthcoming, they are more positive toward organizational programs that could foster their career.

Control over the Means of Goal Achievement. This measure is an attempt to determine the individual's perception of his influence on the allocation of resources required to achieve his goals. It is a measure of perceived discretion. For those with low perceived control, psychological participation is positively related to improvement in boss relations ($r = .41$). However, boss involvement is negatively related to goal success ($r = -.22$). Lack of control over resources means that the subordinate may depend on his boss. When there is high dependence, subordinate influence might positively affect attitudes, but boss involvement may be viewed as pressure. Finally, for those with high control over means, reported increases in goal levels are positively related to satisfaction with the boss ($r = .37$). Those who are satisfied with their boss set higher goals when they have control over resources.

Satisfaction with the Situation. Those less satisfied with their current job situation report lower levels of effort when they are more satisfied with their boss ($r = -.39$). It may be that they are satisfied with their boss because he does not demand much of them.

The level of satisfaction differentially affects the manner in which the boss involvement in the job is related to the perceived level of goal success. For those satisfied with the job situation, boss involvement is negatively related to the perceived degree of goal success ($r = -.27$). For those less satisfied, the level of boss involvement is positively related to perceived goal success ($r = .17$) and to better relationships with the boss ($r = .33$). Thus, boss involvement in the job may produce positive effects for those dissatisfied with the current job assignment.

Job Interest. Those with higher levels of job interest seem to react negatively to more active leadership. For instance, effort increases are negatively related to the time that the boss spends on WPR ($r = -.43$), to higher levels of organizational support for MBO ($r = -.26$), and to satisfaction with the boss ($r = -.29$). The manager who is interested in his work may view leader activity as pressure and react with less effort. Yet, for those with high job interest, the level of boss involvement related to improved relations with the boss ($r = .29$). The boss involvement variable tends to emphasize the extent to which the boss knows, is interested in, or is capable of making judgments about the subordinate's work. It seems to be more job specific than the other measures. It may be that those with high job interest are negatively oriented to specific pressures but react more positively to superior's efforts to involve them in decisions.

Those with low job interest, on the other hand, seem generally (although the correlations are slight) positive toward efforts to implement MBO. For instance, goal success is positively related to psychological participation ($r = .29$), and the boss's time on WPR is related to effort increase ($r = .20$). Boss involvement, however, is negatively related to changes in boss relations for those with low job interest ($r = -.21$). The more interest the boss shows, the less improved their relationship is with him.

The data suggest that for those with high job interest there should be less specific involvement of the boss in the work of the subordinate, and that leader pressure to implement a specific program, like MBO, may have negative effects. Those with low job interest, on the other hand, are more likely to react positively to boss involvement.

Frequency of Job Change. For those in jobs with frequently shifting job demands, the more time the boss spends on MBO, the more strongly improved the relationships with the boss ($r = .45$). Those in more stable jobs, however, report lower levels of effort with increased managerial support for MBO ($r = -.31$) and less goal success with more boss involvement ($r = -.23$). This suggests that in changing job situations, efforts by the superior to clarify goals is desirable. This may be due to the increased job certainty that such behavior generates. However, for those in more stable jobs, high levels of leader activity may be viewed as unnecessary and suggestive that the subordinate is not performing adequately.

Priorities for Self-improvement Goals. Table B–8 indicates that when there are well-defined goal priorities, goal success is related to the time spent on MBO by the superior ($r = .47$), organizational support for the program ($r = .21$), the amount of perceived subordinate participation ($r = .46$), and satisfaction with the boss ($r = .39$). On the other hand, there is no significant relationship between these factors and goal success in cases where goal priorities are not defined. This could suggest that before various positive organizational factors can contribute to goal success, the importance of goals should be well understood. This is somewhat supported by the negative relationships between effort increase and some of the supervisory variables for those who report low goal priorities. Table B–8 also indicates that where goal priorities are not well defined, there is less effort when participation ($r = -.32$), satisfaction with the boss ($r = -.40$), and boss involvement with MBO ($r = -.30$) are all high. Perhaps the lack of goal priorities may produce general job ambiguity, and this may be reinforced and made more salient by increased leader activity and behavior.

DISCUSSION

The analysis of the effects of the boss suggests that there are more likely to be both positive and negative effects resulting from the manager's behavior. Notice, for instance, how the use of moderating variables disclosed relationships (see Table B–8) that would not have been detected from an examination of the correlations presented in Table B–5.

Although the boss's time on MBO is related generally to four of the five criterion variables (see Table B–5), it seems that those with higher levels of interest in their jobs react negatively to managerial activity revolving around MBO. On the other hand, those with frequently changing jobs and with an awareness of goal priorities tend to report positive effects with perceived increases in the time that the boss spends on MBO. Those who need certainty, or who are unsure of the environment, tend to report improved relationships with their boss when they believe that the boss is expending effort on MBO. Behavior supportive of MBO is more important for those in relatively more changing, uncertain positions and reinforces situations where goal priorities have been set.

Increased levels of organizational support for MBO resulted in perceived reduction of effort for those with high job interest and those in more stable jobs. It could be that in more certain or stable situations, perhaps those in which the individual is fairly familiar with the job demands, a manager reacts negatively when he feels constrained and pressured to apply MBO. On the other hand, organizational support had positive effects for those who were aware of goal priorities.

The effect of participation was not as generally pervasive as one might have expected from the strong voice of its proponents. For the over-all sample, participation was correlated with improvements in boss relations ($r = .25$, Table B–5). However, the use of moderating variables disclosed other, more meaningful relationships. For instance, higher participation was related to higher satisfaction with MBO for the high-initiative managers. But it had a far greater positive effect for managers who had a high need for policy, and low control over the means of goal priorities. Perhaps, then, as with the other supervisory variables, the most substantial effect of participation occurs in cases where there is a higher need for certainty.

The effect of participation was negative for those who had low goal priorities. Increasing participation may have simply increased the ambiguity and uncertainty already existing.

Satisfaction with the boss was positively correlated with the end-result variables for those with high control over the means of goal achievement and for those who had some awareness of the boss's priorities on self-improvement goals. Negative relationships were noted between satisfaction and the end-result variables for those with high job interest, lower satisfaction with the situation, and for those who had less awareness of goal priorities. Satisfaction with the boss may be reinforcing for those in relatively secure situations, but it may induce ambiguity, ambivalence, and negative results when other environmental conditions are not desirable.

Boss involvement also results in different effects. Negative relationships with the criteria were noted for those with high need for policy, low job interest, low control over means, high satisfaction with the situation, less frequent job changes, and low awareness of boss priorities. Positive effects were found for those with high initiative and high job interest, although involvement by the superior can be negative for those who might view it as a threat to change the status quo.

CONCLUSION

The results of this analysis point to the care that the superior must take in working through the objectives process with his subordinates. A blanket approach for all subordinates is obviously a less than desirable strategy; otherwise, if our conclusions are correct, some negative effects will occur.

The all important question, for which some direction can be provided by this research, is: Will the tailoring of goal setting based on the analysis by the manager of different characteristics of the subordinates reduce the negative impact? Our research would support this, although additional research is needed to develop a more definitive answer.

NOTES

1. Carroll, S. J., Jr., and H. L., Jr. Tosi, "The Relationship of Goal Character-istics to the Success of Management by Objectives as Moderated by Personal-ity and Situational Factors," Paper presented at the American Psychological Association Meetings, September 1969.
2. Vroom, V. *Some Personality Determinants of the Effects of Participation.* Englewood Cliffs, N.J.: Prentice-Hall, 1960.

APPENDIX

C

MEAN SCORES OF MBO QUESTIONNAIRE ITEMS FROM TWO ADMINISTRATIONS OF THE SAME QUESTIONNAIRE, AS DISCUSSED IN CHAPTER 3

TABLE C–1   BEFORE–AFTER AVERAGE SCORES FOR JOB CHARACTERISTIC ITEMS

Item	Before (Average Score)	After (Average Score)	†
Control over means of goal achievement	3.62	3.54	.51
Degree of change in job requirements	3.83	3.67	1.24
Frequency of outside contacts	3.40	3.52	1.13
Satisfaction with pay	2.64	2.81	1.26
Would you leave for better pay	3.49	3.68	.59
Relationships between pay and performance	3.59	3.77	1.28
Relationship between pay and promotion	3.65	3.77	.81
Job interest	4.38	.81	.41

TABLE C–2   BEFORE–AFTER AVERAGE SCORES FOR "NEED FOR
              STRUCTURE" ITEMS

Item	Before (Average Score)	After (Average Score)	†
Need for job certainty	4.26	4.16	.70
Need for policy	3.62	3.43	1.10

TABLE C–3   BEFORE–AFTER AVERAGE SCORES FOR GOAL
              CHARACTERISTIC ITEMS

Item	Before (Average Score)	After (Average Score)	†
Difficulty performance goals	2.89	3.23	3.15***
Difficulty self-improvement goals	3.07	3.26	1.55**
Performance goal importance	3.58	3.89	2.28***
Self-improvement goal importance	3.06	3.31	1.87**
Performance goal clarity	3.37	3.63	1.92**
Knowledge of importance—performance goal	3.03	3.26	1.61*
Excessive performance goals	1.59	1.97	2.7***
Change in difficulty (P.G.)	3.76	4.01	1.63*
Change in difficulty (S.I.)	3.32	3.47	1.27
Influence over performance goals	3.07	3.24	1.21
Influence over self-improvement goals	2.57	2.71	.72

*** The after score was significantly higher than the before score at the .001 level of confidence.
** The after score was significantly higher than the before score at the .05 level of confidence.
* The after score was significantly higher than the before score at the .10 level of confidence.

TABLE C–4   BEFORE–AFTER AVERAGE SCORES FOR FEEDBACK ITEMS

Item	Before (Average Score)	After (Average Score)	†
Feedback frequency			
Performance goals	2.43	2.93	3.2***
Self-improvement goals	2.06	2.59	3.7***
Nature of feedback			
Amount of praise vs. criticism	3.58	3.46	.87
Boss concern with failure	3.90	4.05	1.11
Extent of criticism	2.99	3.20	1.51

*** The after score was significantly higher than the before score at the .025 level of confidence.

TABLE C–5   BEFORE–AFTER AVERAGE SCORES FOR SUPERVISORY RELATIONSHIP ITEMS

Item	Before (Average Score)	After (Average Score)	†
General relationships			
Change in relationships with boss	3.48	3.47	.16
Help from boss in job	2.17	2.08	.43
Boss difficulty in measuring performance	2.39	2.31	.45
Boss concern with career	2.03	1.93	.50
Boss feedback on performance	2.22	2.07	.72
Influence over work			
How often does your boss ask your opinion	3.44	3.41	.22
Subordinate influence over decision	3.88	3.88	.08
Satisfaction with boss			
Boss capability	3.95	3.99	.29
Boss capacity to deal with people	3.96	3.88	.48
Satisfaction with boss	3.91	3.93	.13
Superior involvement—MBO			
Boss emphasis on performance goals	2.44	2.64	1.18
Boss time on MBO	2.6	2.87	1.61*

* The after score was significantly higher than the before score at the .10 level of confidence.

TABLE C–6 BEFORE–AFTER AVERAGE SCORES FOR ORGANIZATIONAL SUPPORT OF MBO ITEMS

Item	Before (Average Score)	After (Average Score)	†
Company interest in MBO	3.7	4.51	5.6***
Boss interest in MBO	3.55	3.94	2.38***

*** The after score was significantly higher than the before score at the .025 level of confidence.

TABLE C–7 BEFORE–AFTER AVERAGE SCORES FOR REACTIONS TO MBO ITEMS

Item	Before (Average Score)	After (Average Score)	†
Effort increase	2.60	3.25	4.89***
Performance goal success	3.11	3.13	.19
Self-improvement goal success	3.20	3.11	.63
Satisfaction with MBO	3.16	3.74	3.77***
How applicable to your job	3.17	3.65	3.23***
Help in job from MBO	2.57	3.08	3.07***

*** The after score was significantly higher than the before score at the .025 level of confidence.

APPENDIX

D

AN EFFECTIVE FORM FOR ESTABLISHING GOALS AND REVIEWING PERFORMANCE IN AN MBO PROGRAM

A GUIDE TO OVERALL PERFORMANCE APPRAISAL FOR SALARY-EXEMPT BLACK & DECKER EMPLOYEES*

* All material in this appendix is presented through the courtesy of The Black & Decker Manufacturing Company.

Black & Decker OVERALL PERFORMANCE WORK SHEET

Fiscal Year 19 _____
Grade _____
Age _____
Years With Company _____
Years in Present Job _____

GENERAL INSTRUCTIONS

OBJECTIVES

The four objectives of this Program are to:

1. Help the individual to improve his knowledge and skill.

2. Assure continuing two-way communications between the individual and his immediate supervisor.

3. Convert Black & Decker's goals into targets for the individual.

4. Realistically appraise the individual's performance.

TARGET SETTING PROCEDURES

1. The manager of each division, department or section should meet with his subordinates in a briefing session to discuss the overall targets of the group. Also, the manager should discuss how the group's targets can be converted to targets for each individual.

2. After the briefing session, each individual should review the group's targets and determine what his own targets should be to help the group achieve its overall targets. Then the individual should prepare the first three elements of the Work Sheet, Parts A through C. Each manager should do the same for each individual reporting to him.

3. Finally, the individual should again meet with his manager and mutually agree on his personal and job targets and principal job responsibilities for the next year.

NOTE: Both the manager and the individual will have a copy of the Work Sheet. The individual's copy is his working copy to be used throughout the year. The manager's copy is his working copy and becomes the permanent file copy at the end of the year.

REVIEW AND APPRAISAL

During the year the manager should hold periodic meetings with the individual to review target progress, discuss any help or assistance needed to achieve a target and make any target changes necessary.

At year-end the manager completes Parts A through E, evaluating how well the individual performed. Then he should meet with the individual to discuss the overall performance appraisal.

WHAT IS THE PURPOSE OF THIS JOB IN TERMS OF THE CONTRIBUTION IT SHOULD MAKE TO THE BUSINESS?

_____
_____
_____

A | Instructions

1. Describe, as specifically as possible, the type of work this individual desires in the near future (2-3 years) and in the long range.

2. List the individual's personal and professional strengths on which he can build to achieve his future aspirations.

3. Indicate those personal and professional areas where he needs further development.

4. Discuss personal development with the individual and together develop a plan to attempt to attain his objectives. Then select a few personal targets which will increase his present knowledge, skills and potential to help him achieve his career aspirations.

NOTE: These targets should largely be determined by the factors that affected the individual's performance last year. . . . see Part D.

A. PERSONAL DEVELOPMENT

1. Career Aspirations: _____
_____
_____
_____

2. Areas of Greatest Strengths: _____
_____
_____
_____
_____

3. Areas Requiring Further Development: _____
_____
_____
_____

4. Personal Targets for the Year	How Well Were Targets Accomplished?

195

B. PRINCIPAL JOB RESPONSIBILITIES

C. SPECIFIC JOB TARGETS   1st Quarter Review

D. OTHER FACTORS AFFECTING JOB PERFORMANCE

HOW WELL DID HE PERFORM?

2nd Quarter Review	3rd Quarter Review	4th Quarter Review	Results

DESCRIBE AND GIVE EXAMPLES

E. OVERALL PERFORMANCE SUMMARY

To be completed by
the manager:

1. Check the statement
   which best describes
   the individual's over-
   all job performance.

1. HOW WELL DID HE MEET STANDARDS OF JOB PERFORMANCE?

_____FAR EXCEEDS: Outstanding Performance in Present Assignment in <u>practically every</u> respect.

_____EXCEEDS: Above Average Perfomance in Present Assignment in <u>most</u> respects.

──────────── ─────────*baseline performance level*────────────

_____MEETS NORMAL REQUIREMENTS: Average or Satisfactory Performance in PRIMARY FUNCTIONS, JOB TASKS and MANNER.

────────────────*baseline performance level*────────────

_____MEETS MINIMUM REQUIREMENTS: Acceptable but does not meet average performance in the majority of primary functions, job tasks and manner.

2. EXPLAIN IN DETAIL:

2. Then support this
   performance rating by
   giving a word picture
   of the individual's
   performance.

3. Review the individ-
   ual's career aspira-
   tions on page one.
   Then, based on pres-
   ent performance and
   overall growth poten-
   tial, recommend a
   career path or future
   jobs you feel the in-
   dividual is capable of
   achieving. It will be
   helpful to consult with
   other managers in oth-
   er divisions for their
   opinions about the in-
   dividual's performance
   and potential.

3. CAREER PATH RECOMMENDATIONS:

NOTE:
   All factors in this
   overall performance
   appraisal should be
   considered when pre-
   paring next year's targets for the individual.

If the individual or the
rater's superior would
like to comment on this
appraisal, attach his
statement to the com-
pleted Work Sheet.

SIGNATURES:

Individual Rated_____ Date_____ ____

Rater_____ Date_____

Rater's Superior_____ Date_____

☐ SEE ATTACHED STATEMENT

Form No. 2283

II. INTRODUCTION TO THE OVERALL PERFORMANCE WORK SHEET*

The top of the first page of the Work Sheet identifies and provides for:

- Employee's Personal Data.
- General Instructions for Work Sheet.
- Purpose of Employee's Job.

The box at the top of the Work Sheet is for the employee's name and job title (addressograph plate). Other identification includes: fiscal year performance period; salary grade; age; years with company and the years in present job. This section is to be completed by the manager before the review period.

The General Instructions include the overall objectives of the program, how to set targets, and the general procedures for review and appraisal.

Next, to identify the purpose of the individual's job, the manager with the individual should state the reason for the job, and what specific contribution(s) it must make to ensure the continued success and growth of the company.

Here are some examples to serve as *guides* in answering this question.

Production (Machining Supervisor)

Ensure that established Black & Decker standards of service, supply, quality, and costs are maintained on all parts scheduled through his area.

R & D (Project Engineer)

Ensure that the necessary engineering development is applied to a product concept. He contributes by meeting Black & Decker's criteria for product-ability, marketability, and profitability.

Marketing (Sales Representative)

To ensure that the company's products are sold within the policies and procedures of his Marketing Division and to meet and/or surpass territorial sales objectives established by management to ensure the continued growth of the company.

Controller (Credit Manager)

To optimize return on investment on accounts receivable.

* [Part I has been omitted as unnecessary for our objectives.—S. J. C. & H. L. T.]

III. INSTRUCTIONS AND SUGGESTIONS FOR USING THE OVER-ALL PERFORMANCE WORK SHEET (PARTS A THROUGH E)

PART A: PERSONAL DEVELOPMENT

The process of effective personal development begins within the individual. Yet one of the primary functions of every manager is to develop his people to achieve their full potential. As a matter of fact, one of the measures of a good manager is how well he develops his people. This is a continuous task for each manager and is necessary to provide for the future growth of the Company.

1. *Career Aspirations*

Before completing question 1 of this part, the manager and the individual should consider the following:

What the manager should do:

   a. *Discuss* with the individual: future Company needs, what part this individual's function could play in the future, and other factors that could affect his career choice.
   b. *Assist* the individual to identify his career goals.
   c. *Relate* Company career opportunities to personal development, and review educational programs that are available to employees.

What the individual should do:

   a. *Identify* his career goals.
   b. *Relate* his personal goals to Black & Decker goals.
   c. *Assume* the primary responsibility for his professional development.

2. *Areas of Greatest Strengths:*

3. *Areas Requiring Further Development:*
                    (Work on 2 and 3 simultaneously.)

The manager and the individual should discuss and then list the individual's greatest strengths and specific weaknesses.

4. *Personal Targets for the Year: How Well Were Targets Accomplished?*

After completing questions 1–3, the manager and the individual should discuss and together develop a *plan* for the employee's continued growth.

The manager is in the best position to help the individual determine his needs. He should also assist in establishing the plan that best fits the individual's needs, but the individual must take the responsibility to set this plan into motion. So, personal development begins with the individual but can best be accomplished with the manager's counsel and guidance.

From the development plan, the manager and the individual then select a few specific targets for the coming year that will increase the individual's present knowledge, skills, and potential, and help him achieve his career aspirations.

PART B: PRINCIPAL JOB RESPONSIBILITIES

The purpose of this section is to identify (and subsequently evaluate) the major *responsibilities* and functions that pertain *only* to the professional, technical, or technological aspects of the individual's job. They are not the managerial or supervisory responsibilities, e.g., organizing, planning, directing, controlling, communications, etc.

Rather, the "Professional, Technical, or Technological" responsibilities are those that are unique to the individual's particular field of work or speciality. For example, a project development engineer's *professional* responsibilities could include researching, designing, testing, evaluating, etc. On the other hand, a training manager's would include "technological" responsibilities that are unique to his job, e.g., researching training needs, designing and producing skills programs, implementing these programs, etc.

NOTE: The managerial/supervisory functions, e.g., planning, organizing, directing, controlling, communicating, etc., pertain to "HOW" an individual gets his job done. These functions apply *equally* to "How he manages himself" and/or "How he manages others." Section D should be used to evaluate these managerial factors, which affect his job performance.

Suggestions:

Review the individual's job responsibilities to develop a current list of all his functions and responsibilities. These are job functions for which the individual is held accountable.

Arrive at a list that both of you understand—one that is *accurate* under *today's*—not yesterday's—condition.

Forget the *detailed* or secondary responsibilities. Stick to the majors.

Here are some examples of Principal Job Responsibilities:

Production (Machining Supervisor)

- Meets scheduled production requirements.
- Meets quality specifications.
- Ensures high level of employee relations.
- Meets budget standards.
- Ensures maximum use of man power, equipment, and materials.

R & D (Project Engineer)

- Provides the functional appropriateness of the product through research and design.
- Ensures an established level of product through testing and evaluating.
- Works with Production Engineering to make sure that product can be produced economically.
- Works with Industrial Design to ensure that product is designed for the end user and has marketable appearance.
- Works with the appropriate Marketing Division to provide product acceptability.
- Develops the drawings, specifications, and parts lists that define the product.

Marketing (Sales Representative)

- Develops and maintains a regular and increasing profitable sales volume of the Division products in his territory.
- Provides marketing advice, training, and service to existing and new company customers.
- Interprets and applies all company policies and programs.

Controller (Credit Manager)

- Investigate, appraise, approve credit of new accounts.
- Provide for systematic collection and follow-up of delinquent accounts.
- Participate in formulation of departmental policy.
- Constantly review existing procedures and innovate new procedures, making every effort to control and reduce department operating costs.

PART C: SPECIFIC JOB TARGETS

Before completing this part,

1. The manager of each division, department, or section should meet with his subordinates in a briefing session to discuss the overall targets of the group. Also, the manager should discuss how the group's targets can be converted to targets for each individual.

2. After the briefing session, each individual should review the group's targets and determine what his own targets should be to help the group achieve its overall targets. Then the manager and the individual should separately rough in Parts A through C. Both should establish targets that are realistic and attainable yet that will enrich, reward, and stretch the individual's potential and capabilities.

3. Finally, the individual should again meet with his manager and establish in writing the individual's personal and job targets and principal job responsibilities for the next year.

NOTE: It may be necessary to modify specific targets or priorities during the year because of unexpected changes in the work load or emphasis on a particular part or function. Flexibility is an essential ingredient in any target. Targets must be treated as flexible guidelines rather than hard-and-fast rules. They must have built in safeguards to allow for quick change should anything go wrong.

Space is provided on the work sheet for this flexibility.

Here are some partial examples of Job Target-Setting:

Production (Machining Supervisor)

1. To attain a minimum of 80% time reduction (Fiscal '69)

   - By Use of Dovetail Form Tools.
   - By Increased Machine Utilization.

2. Train backup man for my job (July 1969)

   - Reading—Management Book.
   - Seminar.
   - Personal On-Job Training.

3. Etc.

R & D (Project Engineer)

1. Make field trips to at least three key market areas and observe this class of product in use in a variety of applications. Submit report by June 1.

2. Create at least two demonstrable functional features not now available on competitive units in this product class (August 15).

3. Reduce first audit drawing errors by 20% compared with those recorded on Project "W" (September 1).

4. Submit a report analyzing the potential for accessory devices with this class of product by November 15.

5. Etc.

Marketing (Sales Representative)

1. Increase ratio of accessory sales to tools in my territory from _____ % to _____ % by September 30, 19__.

2. Increase average number of calls per day in my territory from _____ to _____ by March 25, 19__.

3. Eliminate the marginal accounts (under $X.00 per year volume;) add number of new distributors, one each in (*town*), (*city*), etc.

4. Etc.

Controller (Credit Manager)

1. Recommend organization requirements in conjunction with manager of accounts receivable in anticipation of mechanization of receivable and credit functions, by November 1, 1968, with the goal of reducing 10 clerical jobs, redirecting funds to more professional personnel, for an increase of 3 people (net of 7). Net dollars saved: $25,000 annually. Totally implemented by September 30, 1969.

2. Make study to determine possible alternatives to present dating terms; rough draft by December 31; finished, April 30. Goal: To reduce average receivables to 15% of sales with no dilution of operating profit by September 30, 1969, with ultimate goal of 13.0% by September 30, 1970.

3. Establish and maintain goal of limiting bad debts to 1.3% of sales.

4. Establish dollar limit of $50,000 in expense accounts and maintain within that limit.

5. Evaluate personnel and select at least two for training with the goal of providing one backup man for my present job, by June 1.

6. Etc.

PART D: OTHER FACTORS AFFECTING JOB PERFORMANCE

As stated in the work sheet instructions, this section is to be completed at the end of the year before the individual's review.

Before completing this section, the manager should critically analyze the *way* in which the individual accomplished his targets and responsibilities for the review period. Also include in this analysis the knowledge the man brings to the job, his technical and managerial skills, and his personal character- istics. To assist you in this analysis some factors are listed below that could affect overall preformance. The following are only examples of a list of factors that might be considered.

Leadership. Gets understanding, support, and effective action of others; gets things done through other people; inspires respect and commitment to objectives; takes charge; encourages others to use their own initiative and talents; forceful, but not domineering.

Organizing ability. Divides up job into manageable parts; assigns action roles and delegates; follows up; sees that goals and deadlines are met; decisive; gets right people in right roles; builds strong organization; makes effective use of materials, manpower, time, and money.

Forward planning ability. Anticipates problems and looks ahead; plans action steps in timely sequences; sets appropriate priorities; develops alternative courses of action to meet various eventualities.

Analytical ability. Grasps complicated concepts; can see the problem and work out the answer; intelligent.

Judgment. Ability to weigh and evaluate; separates important from unimportant; assesses probable consequences and proves to have been right; has common sense; not taken in by wishful thinking or un- warranted enthusiasm.

Quantity of work. Works hard; doesn't quit until job is finished; always ready to take on more; has efficient work habits.

Reliability. Ties up loose ends; doesn't require follow-up; gets things done without mistakes; does what he says he will do; available when needed; meets assignments and schedules on time; performs well under stress; has guts.

Creativeness. Develops new ideas, concepts, solutions; an opportunity finder.

Experience. Knows his specialty; knows other aspects of business and other important disciplines; has been around and knows what's what; competent.

Breadth of interest. Keeps abreast of outside developments; seeks and acquires new knowledge; a good learner; broadens personal horizons into other worthwhile fields; interests himself in good citizenship and other good works; sees his job and his company in its broadest perspective.

Adaptability to change. Has open mind to new ideas; adaptable to new situations; seeks opportunity in change; willing to give new ideas a fair trial.

Cooperation. Accepts supervision; appreciates and works toward best interests of the whole; respects and cooperates with others; personal objectives compatible with company objectives.

Communication ability. Organizes and articulates information well and takes action to disseminate it appropriately; his associates understand his ideas, statements, objectives, conclusions; sells his position effectively both orally and in writing.

Business sense. Ability to make money; senses the future; spots the good opportunities; an entrepreneur, a shrewd judge of values, a good negotiator.

Empathy. Perceives real meanings and feelings of others; a good listener; intuitive toward different kinds of people; knows how to handle people of varying types and personalities; considerate and tactful.

Training ability. Trains and develops subordinates effectively; appraises and counsels subordinates effectively; develops replacements; moves high potential personnel into higher challenge jobs; uses variety of training methods; willing to part with good people from own department.

Ability to appraise people. A good judge of character; accurately appraises abilities of others; selects on basis of ability to do the job.

Motivation and initiative. Ambitions for a successful career; works for personal growth and advancement; willingly accepts responsibility; energetic; a self-starter; gets on with things without prodding; sees what has to be done and does it; has guts to tackle a tough assignment.

*   *   *

Appearance and behavior. Has good personal reputation; likeable; makes good impression; a credit to the company.

Standards. Has high moral standards; his ethics, conduct, word can be relied on; gains trust and confidence of others; treats everyone fairly, and justly; thoughtful of best interests of the organization (time, money materials); intellectually honest; tells boss his true opinions.

The manager should select those factors that he feels most adversely affected the individual's performance last year, describe them, and give examples in the space provided.

Important: During this analysis the manager should also select a few factors that he feels are solid strengths on which the individual should capitalize. This will help the manager and the individual when completing Part A of the Work Sheet (Personal Development) for the next year.

PART E: OVERALL PERFORMANCE SUMMARY

The purpose of this section is to summarize the overall performance of the individual. Before completing this part the manager should:

1. Read the instructions on the Work Sheet, Part E.

2. Review all preceding parts to crystallize his thoughts about the individual's total performance.

3. Then give a complete word picture of the individual's performance.

Procedures for completing this part:

a. The appraiser completes Part E.

b. Before reviewing the Work Sheet with the individual, the manager should discuss the summary with his immediate superior to obtain his thoughts.

c. Then the manager meets with the individual and discusses his overall performance for the *previous* year. After appraising the individual's previous performance, the manager and the individual begin completing Parts A through C for the *next year's* Work Sheet.

d. The manager then sends the completed copy of the Work Sheet to Personnel for retention in the individual's personal folder.

IV. QUESTIONS FREQUENTLY ASKED ABOUT PERFORMANCE APPRAISALS

1. QUESTION: *What do you mean by saying the Overall Performance Work Sheet is a "Working Tool"?*

   Answer:

   a. The Work Sheet should be used constantly—weekly, monthly, and at least quarterly. The manager and the individual use it together.

   b. It is not to be thought of as a formal, awesome device to punish or reprimand people. It should be a "Working Tool" to help the individual in doing his job and provide opportunity for his continued growth.

   c. Notes can be freely made on the Work Sheet and additional sheets and memos can be attached.

2. QUESTION: *Should a manager use his subordinate's Work Sheets when working with his own superior?*

   Answer:

   The manager will find his people's Work Sheet helpful to:

   a. Improve communication upward through the division.

   b. Give his superior the opportunity to provide specific counsel and aid in setting and changing targets.

3. QUESTION: *Should salary be mentioned during a performance review?*

   Answer:

   No, Black & Decker believes this is *not* the most effective way for a manager to motivate an employee to improve his performance and stimulate him to take action for his personal growth.
   Performance Reviews should always be held annually, on a schedules basis prior to a new fiscal year.

Salary Reviews should always be held at a *different* time of the year from Performance Reviews—never at the same time.

Why? If a Salary Review is at a *fixed* and expected (by the individual) time, one of two things happens:

1. If you don't give him a raise when he expects it, he's resentful.

2. If you do give him a raise, he expected it and felt he deserved it. In this case he's not motivated for future improved performance.

4. QUESTION: *When should a manager seek the help of others in making employee appraisals?*

Answer:

At Black & Decker, all performance appraisals should be discussed and reviewed by the appraiser's superior before the actual appraisal is held with the employee. This is recommended for a number of reasons:

a. If the appraiser is a new manager, he may need input from someone who has worked with or supervised the employee previously.

b. If the individual has had a working relationship with people in other divisions, it will also be helpful in obtaining their opinion.

c. The danger of personal bias or prejudices will be less.

d. It makes the appraisal more objective.

e. If the relationship with an employee is not the best, an assist from the appraiser's superior may help overcome an interpersonal relations problem.

5. QUESTION: *After the manager and his superior have agreed on an individual's appraisal, does the completed appraisal form become a "hard and fast" document when reviewing it with the individual?*

Answer:

No, a manager should keep an open mind when he discusses the overall performance appraisal with the individual. The manager should expect some sort of response from the individual—there should be no surprises if the relationship with the individual is sound. If, however, in discussing the appraisal with the individual, the manager discovers new information about the man's performance, or if he has not given proper weight to a factor, then he should be willing to modify the appraisal appropriately.

INDEXES

Author Index

Pages have sometimes been given for authors who are mentioned on the text page only by note number. In these cases, the "Notes" at the end of the chapter will have to be consulted.

211

Subject Index

Budget constraints, 86, 109
Budgeting process and MBO, 108–12
  problems, 108
  subordinate participation, 112
  timing problem, 110–12

Cascading process of setting goals, 56–58, 71
Change(s)
  in reaction to MBO, 65
  required by objectives, 70
Change program, the, 61–62
Coaching, 114, 138
Commitment of top management to MBO, 44
Compensation, 116–19
  goal achievement and, 118
  internal wage administration, 119
  performance level and, 116–17
  as reward, 116–17, 119
  timing of salary decision, 118–19
Consultants, 59–60
Control standards, 132
Coordinating requirements and contingencies, 82
Criteria measures, 34
Criticism, 95–96, 117, 128, 175

Deadlines, 86, 103
Defensive reactions to review, 54, 58, 92
Development
  managerial. See Management development
  personal, 73, 76–79
  of personnel, 137–38
Disadvantages of MBO. See also Management by objectives: problems in use of
  perceived, 26–27
Discretion and objectives, 74–75

Effectiveness of MBO, 14–15, 121–23
  research on, 121–22
Effort increase, 125, 180. See also Performance: changes in
English studies on MBO, 12–13, 107, 141
Evaluation. See also Performance review
  of goal accomplishment, 102–103
  problems, 82–85, 101

Failure
  sense of, 104
  superior concern about, 173, 174, 177
Feedback. See also Performance review
  characteristics, 181
    change in, 64
  effects of, 5–7
  frequency of, 42, 65
    attitude towards MBO, and, 179
    effort and, 177

goal clarity and, 167, 174
  managerial factors and, 181–82
  superior–subordinate relationship and, 181–82
performance improvement and, 116
Follow-up on implementation, 59–60
Frustration, 96–97
Functional interdependency, 101

General Electric studies, 6, 8–10, 96, 104, 122, 132
Ghiselli Self-Descriptive Inventory, 34, 125, 162–63, 175
Goal(s). See also Objectives
  clarity, 167, 174, 182
  distortion of, 15
  establishment of, 71. See also Goal setting
    cascading process, 56–58, 71
  failure, 174, 177
  hard vs. soft, 83
  relative importance of, 103
  statement of. See Statement of goals
  types of, 73–74
    performance objectives, 73, 74–76
    personal development objectives, 73, 76–79
    routine objectives, 84–85
    special project objectives, 84, 85
Goal accomplishment, 173
  causes of lack of, 104
  compensation and, 118
  evaluation of, 102–103
  means to, 103
  success in, 173
Goal characteristics
  anticipated sanctions and, 167
  before-after scores for items of, 190
  change in, 64
  feedback frequency and, 167, 174
  general participation and, 167
  measurement of, 34
  moderating variables and, 167–71
    personality, 168–69
    situational factors, 168, 169–70
  organization support for MBO, and, 167
  perceptions of higher management, and, 167
  research results, 164–72
  satisfaction with superior, and, 167, 182
  superior–subordinate relationship and, 167, 182
  superior's time on MBO, and, 167, 182
Goal orientation, 130
Goal setting, 31–33, 35–36, 53–54, 69–87, 126
  arrangement of meetings for, 61–62
  cascading process, 56–58
  general research findings on, 35–36, 40–42

Negative effects of MBO, 15

Objective appraisal criteria, 135–37
  personality-trait ratings, 135–36
Objectives, 69–70. *See also* Goal(s)
  managerial discretion and, 74–75
  as means–end distinctions, 71–72
  statement of, 55, 72–73
    purpose of, 70–71
  types of, 73–74
    performance objectives, 73, 74–76
    personal development objectives, 73, 76–79
    routine objectives, 84–85
    special project objectives, 84, 85
Organization support: goals and, 167
Organizational characteristics, 123–27
Organizational level and influence, 30–31
Organizational structure, 28–33, 44
Organizational support, 65, 192
Organizational unit and influence, 28–30
Orientation to MBO, 127

Paper-work problems, 15, 44, 52
Participation. *See also* Influence over goals
  in budgeting, 112
  general, 167
  in goal setting, 167
  research on, 7–8
Performance
  changes in, 14
  measurement (or appraisal) of, 15, 34. *See also* Performance review
  problems in, 82–85, 101
Performance objectives, 73, 74–76
Performance review, 89–105. *See also* Feedback
  anxiety and, 93
  behavioral problems during, 90–92. *See also* Behavior
  closing of session, 97–98
  defensive reactions to, 54, 58, 92
  final goal review:
    carrying out of, 102–104
    objectives of, 90
  frequency of, 58–59
  functions of, 112–14
    to evaluate quality of performance, 112–13
    identification of management potential, 112, 113–14
  general guides for, 93–98
  implementation of MBO, and, 48, 58–59
  importance of, 44
  intermediate review:
    carrying out of, 98–102
    objectives of, 89–90
  listening and, 94
  means–end distinctions and, 81, 83

perceptions and, 91
research summary, 36–37, 42–43, 173–80
superior–subordinate relationship in, 128
time allocation for, 99, 100
types of subordinates, and, 99
unwillingness to carry out, 6, 51–52, 99
Personal characteristics, 123–29
Personal development objectives, 73, 76–80
Personality, 125, 169, 175, 176. *See also* Performance review; Superior–subordinate relationships
  Ghiselli Self-Description Inventory, 34, 125, 162–63
  intelligence, 168, 169
  maturity, 168, 169
  measurement of factors of, 34
  self-assurance, 125, 168, 169, 175
    effort and, 125, 169
    participation and, 125
Personality-trait ratings, 135–36
Personnel development, 137–38
Planning, 14, 131
Planning ability: lack of, 50–51
Plans, action, 80–82
Pressures
  psychological, 51
  routine *vs.* non-routine, 101
Problems
  identification of, 137
  in measurement of performance, 82–85, 101
  perceived, 26, 43–44
Process of MBO, 3
Purex studies, 11, 122

Rationale for MBO, 23–24
Research on actual MBO programs, 8–15
  before-after questionnaires, 60–61, 63–64, 149–60
    mean scores compared, 189–92
  Black & Decker, 22–45, 60–61, 63–64, 122, 126, 129, 141, 149–60, 164-88, 189-92
    format for goal setting and review, 193–209
  discussion of, 14–15
  English studies, 12–13, 107, 141
  General Electric studies, 6, 8–10, 96, 104, 122, 132
  hospital study, 13–14
  Mendleson study, 12
  Raia (Purex) studies, 11, 122
  University of Kentucky studies, 10
Research following implementation, 60–67
Research foundations of MBO, 3–18
  feedback, 5–6